HEAVEN

AS WE KNOW IT
AND
WHY IT MATTERS ON EARTH

By
Anders Bennett

ADISAN Publishing AB

Introduction

I have been there. Patiently and anxiously waiting at the bedside of a loved one in a hospital is a sorrowful experience. The labored breaths are kept in rhythm by the chimes of the machines. Occasionally, one of the hospital staff will come by to ensure the comfort of the patient and the family. However, nothing can relieve the pressure of the moment that is approaching. Whether it is minutes or hours away, death is creeping ever closer.

A million things run through your mind in these situations. You think about all the wonderful moments you had with that loved one. The missed opportunities to spend time with them grip you with guilt. The practical burden of the days to come begins to weigh on you. This is not to forget the overwhelming sadness that ebbs and flows through it all. Amidst the sorrow, one inevitable question is raised, "What happens next?" As the breathing begins to slow and the devices begin to wind down, what will happen to that loved one next?

There are many proposed answers to this question (some of which will be addressed in this book), but according to the Bible, there are only two possibilities. For all who have placed their faith in Jesus, Heaven is their eternal home after death. Those who lack faith are subjected to the eternal punishment they have earned in Hell. Gallons of ink and mountains of paper have been used in the contemplation and speculation of what these eternal realities will be like. In this book, the efforts of the writer will remain focused on Heaven.

Heaven is the only true comfort for the dying patient and the waiting family. For those who believe, the hope of it becomes their motivation in everyday life. Heaven as we know it greatly impacts how we live on earth. The goal of this book is to inspire the hope of the believer and call them to live in light of it. When asked by His disciples how to pray, Jesus gave them a model to follow. The famous prayer goes like this:

Our Father in heaven, hallowed be your name. Your kingdom come, your will be done, on earth as it is in heaven. Give us this day our daily bread, and forgive us our debts, as we also have forgiven our debtors. And lead us not into temptation, but deliver us from evil.

The central aim of this book is to unpack the full sense of what Jesus taught us to pray for. The depths of what it means for God's will to be done on earth as it is in Heaven will change the way you view your purpose in life today, tomorrow, and for all of eternity.

In order to do that well, we must know what Heaven is like according to the Scriptures. Throughout the course of this book, we will take a thorough look at the topic from various angles. In the first chapter, we will wrestle with the question surrounding life after death. We will consider some of the proposed answers in society today, and we will contrast those ideas against what the Bible teaches.

In Chapter 2, we will work our way through one of Jesus' teachings regarding Heaven. He says that it is easier for a camel to go through the eye of a needle than for a rich person to enter the kingdom of God. How impossible is it for us to get to Heaven? Is there any hope? Together, we will find the answer that the Bible provides on the topic.

Next, we will look at the various views of Heaven that have been presented throughout history. In pop culture, we get views of heaven that include cloudy floors and winged babies playing harps. In the history of the Church, there have been all kinds of visions of our heavenly home presented. We will take an overview look at the origins and errors of these views in Chapters 3 and 4.

In Chapters 5 through 7, we will dive into the Word of God and see what it plainly says about Heaven. The fifth chapter will cover the central teaching of the Old Testament. In the sixth, we will look at what Jesus said about the place He is preparing for His people. And finally, in the seventh chapter, we will look at the continued teachings on Heaven from the apostles of Christ.

In Chapter 8, we will settle down in the book of Revelation and view the vision of the apostle John of the Present Heaven. The distinction between the Present Heaven and the New Heaven to come will be made and defended here, too.

In Chapters 9 through 11, we will enjoy Jesus' statement in Revelation that all things will be made new by Him. In the final chapters of the climactic ending of Scripture, the New Heaven, New Earth, and New Jerusalem are all introduced. We will savor those pages as they point to the glorious beginning of eternity.

As you read your way through this book, more questions may come into your mind than are answered in each chapter. There is no way to predict or address every question in one volume, but the most common questions that haven't already been addressed will be taken point by point in Chapter 12.

Finally, it would be irresponsible to view the glories of Heaven without reckoning with the reality of its horrible counterpart. If Heaven is the reward of all who are saved, what exactly are they being saved from? What is the punishment for dying without faith in Jesus? The place called Hell will be briefly addressed in the thirteenth chapter.

As the perfect Paradise is studied from chapter to chapter, there will be a section entitled "On Earth As It Is In Heaven." Under this heading, all of the examinations of that chapter will be taken out of the theoretical and planted firmly into your life. As James says, we are to be hearers and doers of God's Word. This means that what we know of Heaven affects how we live on Earth. So, each chapter will end with some thoughts on how to apply that chapter to your life today.

Also, study help is included at the end of each chapter. There will be a list of Scriptures that are referenced and some suggestions for further reading on the subject. There will also be a list of discussion questions that can help you study this book with a friend or in a small group.

Heaven is too glorious a subject to be ignored and too important a subject to be taken lightly. As you make your way through this, I hope you'll do it with a prayerful heart that asks the Lord to give you glimpses of Home. As He does, through the medium of His Word, may each image affect your life for your good and His glory.

CHAPTER 1

LIFE AFTER DEATH

Ever since Genesis 3, death has been a terrible reality of life. God made it clear to Adam and Eve that if they broke His Law, death would be their punishment (Genesis 2:17). The Devil slithered onto the scene and planted the seed of doubt in Eve's mind by asking, "Did God really say you would die?" With the bitter bite of whatever fruit came from the tree of the knowledge of good and evil, Adam and Eve sinned and brought the curse of death along with it. From that moment, their biological clocks began ticking. They had their first night of restless sleep and woke up with their first bout of soreness. Death was coming, which raises the question we all ask at some point in life, "What happens after death?"

Part of the answer must be found in the design of life before The Fall. When God created all things, including men and women, did He design any of them to die? The animals were to be under the dominion of man, but not in their stomachs (Genesis 1:28-30). Death was not to come to them by the hand of man, and we have no indication that it would come to them at all. The same is true for men. If death was the punishment for sin, that means everlasting life was supposed to be the normal reality.

Our mind, body, and soul were all designed to live forever. These individuals had never been faced with this cold, hard truth of death before. All they had known (perhaps for years) about life was eternal, perfect bliss. They were never in need. Hunger pains were foreign to them. Even the work they did in the garden was comparatively effortless. The family they were going to have was going to come to them pain-free. Blisters, sores, and boils were unknown to them. The Garden of Eden was the truest Paradise ever to be known. But now their bodies are in danger, and there must be concern for their souls, too. When sin entered into the world, and death by sin, that design was disrupted. Mind and body are clearly in jeopardy. Death would put them to an end. But what happens to the soul? Can something physical end the spiritual? Are our lungs and hearts connected to our souls in that way?

The whole Bible assumes, and oftentimes explicitly says, that there is life after death. In fact, not long after Adam and Eve are kicked out of the Garden of Eden, we see an example of this idea.

Cain spoke to Abel his brother. And when they were in the field, Cain rose up against his brother Abel and killed him. Then the Lord said to Cain, "Where is Abel your brother?" He said, "I do not know; am I my brother's keeper?" And the Lord said, "What have you done? The voice of your brother's blood is crying to me from the ground.

Genesis 4:8-10, ESV

Adam and Eve's child, Cain, brings death to his brother, Abel. The way God addresses this sin with Cain sheds light on the subject. He says that Abel's blood cries out from the ground. We know that that's not literal. It is a figurative way of saying that there has been an injustice that must be rectified. But what justice could Abel be longing for if death ended all existence? What could his blood be crying out for if there was nothing after his murder? God speaks of Abel as someone who still exists in some way, even after his murder. Abel's soul, now safely in the hands of God, still deserved the dignity of justice. This concept of life after death appears in every book of the Bible.

Life after death clearly has a spiritual component, but what does the Bible actually say it will be like? Some religions teach that our soul is reincarnated here on earth as a physical being. Others will teach that our souls lose their personal identity and are absorbed into God. Still, some others will teach that our souls will exist in perfect peace, but the parameters of what that looks like are undefined. For our purposes, we're going to focus on what the Bible teaches about what happens to our souls after death.

Many times, the Bible describes death as sleep (Daniel 12:2; 1 Thessalonians 4:15-17). This could lead to the conclusion that the soul sleeps within the body until the day Jesus returns and brings a great resurrection of the dead. One such example of this idea could be found in the resurrection of Lazarus.

Lazarus was a dear friend of Jesus. There came a time when he was desperately sick, so his family sent word to Jesus. They called on Him to come and heal Lazarus (John 11:3). However, Lazarus died before Jesus could arrive (John 11:13-14). Jesus finally makes it to the home of his deceased friend. He mourns over the loss and then works a miracle. He goes to the tomb of Lazarus and tells the dead man to rise (John 11:43). In an incredible display of God's power, Lazarus walks out from the tomb (John 11:44). This poses an interesting question when thinking about life after death. What happened to the soul of Lazarus in the meantime? Did he go to Heaven and then get sent back? Did his soul hang out in the tomb for a few days until Jesus came?

Some theologians would say this story supports a concept called soul sleep. This is the idea that our souls go into a dormant state after our death. They will be awoken again at the resurrection of every person when Jesus returns. Does this example prove the soul sleep theory? Lazarus had clearly died. Before the great resurrection at the return of Christ, he was raised. Mind, body, and soul were all intact. When he arose, there was no recording of him speaking about Heaven (which would be hard to remain silent about). Could it be that his soul was simply dormant in his body until it was rejuvenated?

There are a few reasons why we can reasonably say that the concept of soul sleep is not taught in the Bible. The first comes from a practical issue. The resurrection of a body within days of its death is a rare occurrence. So, to rely on the story of Lazarus would only present an exception to any rule. It is certainly possible for God to have treated the death of Lazarus differently, considering He had sent His Son to raise him from the dead. However, this cannot be reliably treated as the typical case study.

Most bodies that have been laid to rest have decayed to the point that they barely exist. There are many bodies that have been lost in fires, digested by animals, and drifted into the sea. Could soul sleep be a viable theory if the mind and body are gone? Granted, the Lord can do whatever He wants. But there is a clearer answer presented in Scripture.

Paul writes a very helpful sentence in 2 Corinthians 2:8. He says, "Yes, we are of good courage, and we would rather be away from the body and at home with the Lord." In this verse, it is made clear that our souls only exist in two locations. They either occupy our body while we are alive on this earth, or they occupy our eternal residence (either in Heaven or Hell). There is no middle ground presented. This means that when we die physically, our souls continue to live on. This leads us to the next big idea we find in Scripture about life after death. Our souls live eternally.

OUR SOULS LIVE ETERNALLY

Jesus speaks on the subject of life after death many times in His ministry. Concerning the soul, He has a challenging and encouraging truth for them to consider as persecution comes.

And do not fear those who kill the body but cannot kill the soul. Rather fear him who can destroy both soul and body in hell.

Matthew 10:28, ESV

According to Jesus, no person can kill our souls. This also implies that no angel or demon has the power to destroy souls either. There is only one with that ability. It is God who is the Creator of our souls. And He alone has the power to destroy them. This means that, apart from God's intervention, our souls are eternal. Whatever life after death looks like, it is one that lasts forever. We will address whether or not God does destroy souls in Hell in a ladder chapter.

This point is further expressed as Jesus speaks about the rewards for those who place their faith in Him and the punishment for those who do not. In Matthew 25:31-46, Jesus describes the final judgment that will take place when He returns. On that day, every person will stand before Him and be divided into sheep (believers) and goats (non-believers). The believers will be given the reward of entering into the Kingdom of God that lasts forever (Psalm 145:13), and the non-believers will be sent into the eternal fire. This section concludes with a summary statement that calls the Kingdom of God an eternal reward of life and the fire an eternal punishment. It is clear that Jesus' view of the soul of man is that it lives eternally.

Our Souls Will Be Reunited With Our Bodies

There is one more important thing to consider about life after death. According to the Bible, there will be a great resurrection day for all people. Our bodies, whether wholly intact like Lazarus or destroyed by fire like the citizens of Sodom and Gomorrah, will be raised, reconstructed, and reconstituted with our souls. Revelation 20:11-15 describes this day with apocalyptic language. It teaches that all men will be raised back to life and stand judgment before the Great White Throne of God. Paul gives a more theologically driven description of that day in his letter to the church in Corinth. There, he says,

So is it with the resurrection of the dead. What is sown is perishable; what is raised is imperishable. It is sown in dishonor; it is raised in glory. It is sown in weakness; it is raised in power. It is sown a natural body; it is raised a spiritual body. If there is a natural body, there is also a spiritual body.

1 Corinthians 15:42-44, ESV

In a later chapter, we will consider all of the wonders of these verses and the new bodies that will be raised at the return of Christ. For now, we will focus on the soul's place in all of this. What is clear from this passage is that our souls will be reunited with our physical bodies.

God has a plan for life after death. He has not needlessly nor carelessly given every human a soul. He has a wonderful redemptive plan for each and every one. The soul that leaves the body in death will either experience eternity with Him or apart from Him. He does not desire anyone to perish apart from Him (2 Peter 3:9). In fact, He would be glorified all the more if everyone were to live with Him forever in Heaven. But we bear the responsibility of placing our faith in His Son.

On Earth As It Is In Heaven

If it is true that we all have immoral, eternal souls, then how we handle them is of massive importance. A cursory reading of the Psalms reveals that our souls heavily affect our lives. Our souls can be troubled (Psalm 6:3), torn apart (Psalm 7:2), crushed with longing (Psalm 119:20), or restored (Psalm 23:3), and guarded (Psalm 25:20). Jesus expresses the importance of the human soul above all other earthly possessions when He posed the question in Mark 8:36, "What does it profit a man to gain the whole world and forfeit his soul?"

These truths of life after death should have a profound impact on our lives before death. Our souls are something worth protecting from harm and strengthening. In regards to protecting our souls from harm, our primary aim should be to resist the temptation towards sin. Sin is the bringer of death, not only to our physical bodies but to our spiritual lives as well. Paul says in Ephesians 2:1 that we are spiritually dead in our trespasses and sins. Once we've been made alive (Ephesians 2:4), we have the holy task of protecting our souls from spiritual harm. Paul goes on to describe that task as a war. In the sixth chapter of the Ephesian church, he tells us to "put on the whole armor of God" because we are in a war against Satanic powers who are aiming fiery darts at us.

What temptations are drawing you in today? Do you realize that with each and every sin, you cause damage to your own soul? If a prisoner had been set free and the jail had been opened, they would never choose to spend the rest of their lives playing with chains. The same ought to be true of the Christian. If we have been freed from the dominion of sin by our faith in Jesus, far be it from us to continue playing with that deadly poison. While we have no need to fear that we will lose our salvation and that our soul is in eternal jeopardy, our dealings with sin can hurt and tarnish our relationship with God. Why else would Paul cry out in Romans 6:1-2, "Are we to continue in sin that grace may abound? By no means! How can we who died to sin still live in it?" I encourage you today to examine your own lifestyle. Take inventory of your actions and your motivations and see what sinfulness still remains. Once you've identified that sin, flee from it. Fight hard against it, for you have a precious soul to protect.

Not only should we do the hard work of protecting our souls, but we should make every effort to strengthen them. According to the Bible, our souls are strengthened by meditating on the Word of God (Psalm 119:28) and investing in our relationship with God (James 4:8). Books like these are of great advantage to the believer because they can shed light on hard parts of the Bible. But they should never replace the steady diet of God's Word and the relationship that is built with Him by prayer and worship.

I would encourage you to set aside time before or after you read a chapter of this book to work on your relationship with God. You can do this by attending a Bible-believing church, reading through a Bible reading plan, singing songs of praise, spending time praying through a prayer journal, etc. The options are endless, but the goal is simple: strengthening the only part of you that is eternal. For what gain is it to you to have incredible physical, financial, or emotional health when you pass from life into death? When your soul leaves your body for the life to come, what will have been the most important use of your earthly time? The unspoken answer to the question of Christ is that all of life is of no value if you do not care for your own soul.

FOR FURTHER STUDY

Read Genesis 1-3

Read John 11:1-44

Read Matthew 25:31-46

Read 1 Thessalonians 4:15-17

Read Revelation 20:11-15

DISCUSSION QUESTIONS

1. What were you taught about life after death growing up?

2. How has your view of life after death changed?

3. What does the Bible teach about life after death?

4. Why did God make our souls eternal?

5. What do you think about the concept of soul sleep?

6. How do you protect your soul from evil?

7. What can you do to strengthen your soul this week?

CHAPTER 2

THE EYE OF THE NEEDLE

Heaven is the eternal destination of God's people. Its beauty is unmatched, and its glory has never been experienced by the living. The longing for such a home brings up the question, "How do we get there?" Like when planning a vacation, at some point, you have to pull out a map and figure out how you're going to make it there. Unlike on a map, however, there are not many routes to the same destination. Once again, as you ask different religions, you'll find a whole host of answers on how to get to their version of Heaven. But what does the Bible say about it? Is Heaven a reality that is too good to be true for descendants of Adam?

Jesus has an encounter with a rich young ruler who is asking these very questions. He wants to know how he can inherit eternal life (Mark 10:17). Jesus' answers to this question give us a clear road map to Heaven. Let's take a look.

And as he was setting out on his journey, a man ran up and knelt before him and asked him, "Good Teacher, what must I do to inherit eternal life?" And Jesus said to him, "Why do you call me good? No one is good except God alone. You know the commandments: 'Do not murder, Do not commit adultery, Do not steal, Do not bear false witness, Do not defraud, Honor your father and mother.'" And he said to him, "Teacher, all these I have kept from my youth." And Jesus, looking at him, loved him, and said to him, "You lack one thing: go, sell all that you have and give to the poor, and you will have treasure in heaven; and come, follow me." Disheartened by the saying, he went away sorrowful, for he had great possessions.

Mark 10:17-22, ESV

When this young man asked Jesus his question, I suspect he already had an answer in mind. He was assuming that Jesus was going to rattle off the 10 Commandments and see if he had been faithful to keep them. He expected Jesus to judge his worthiness of Heaven by his own goodness. So when Jesus responds with, "No one is good except God alone," it changes the whole tone of the conversation. The credit that the young man was using to buy his ticket to Heaven just got denied.

Jesus goes on to prove His point by saying that the young man already knows the standard the Law has set. The young man puffs out his chest and says that he has kept them all since he was a kid. Jesus could have stopped him right there and put his finger on the fifth commandment to honor your father and mother. There is not a child alive that has done this perfectly, including this young man. However, Jesus overlooks this side problem and places his finger on the central issue.

When Jesus commanded this young man to sell all he had and give it to the poor, He was calling him to destroy his idol. Money and possession controlled his heart. We know this because he walked away sorrowfully and did not follow Jesus. If he had to pick between Jesus as God and money, he chose money. This means that no matter how many good deeds this young man performed, they would never remove the false god on the throne of his heart. Each of his righteous acts had been tainted by sin since they were not done to the glory of God alone.

Before we judge this man too harshly, it would benefit us to see if we pass the test that Jesus delivers. Take a look back over the 10 Commandments in Exodus 20:1-17. Have you fallen short on any of these? Perhaps you would say that you have not murdered anyone or committed adultery. Jesus says that even if you have not done those things physically, hate and lust are equally as damning (Matthew 6:21-30). Give yourself the benefit of the doubt for a moment and say that you have not had that level of hate or lust in your heart. Have you ever lied, coveted, or stolen something petty? What about honoring your father and mother? Were your childhood days full of perfect obedience?

Jesus is surely right when He said that no one is good. There is no level of goodness or righteousness that we can achieve that will buy our ticket to Heaven. If God is pure and holy, He is unable to dwell with sin (Psalm 5:4). He cannot leave it unpunished (Exodus 34:7). If we were to enter into His presence with even a spot of sin on our record, we would be cast out of His paradise like Adam and Eve (1 Corinthians 6:9-10). This young man's riches had clouded his mind and darkened his heart to the truth. He was a sinner in need of a Savior.

A Hard Message To Hear

After this interaction, Jesus looks to His disciples and describes the young man's desperate situation by saying,

And Jesus looked around and said to his disciples, "How difficult it will be for those who have wealth to enter the kingdom of God!" And the disciples were amazed at his words. But Jesus said to them again, "Children, how difficult it is to enter the kingdom of God! It is easier for a camel to go through the eye of a needle than for a rich person to enter the kingdom of God." And they were exceedingly astonished, and said to him, "Then who can be saved?" Jesus looked at them and said, "With man it is impossible, but not with God. For all things are possible with God."

Mark 10:23-27, ESV

Jesus' indictment of the rich is applicable to all mankind. This seems to be a particular challenge for the rich, for they tend to feel less need for God. Consider the poor beggar on the side of the road. They do not know where their next meal will come from or where they will sleep from day to day. They are always dependent on others. When they hear the message that they must depend on God for their salvation, it makes sense to them.

Take the rich man in the mansion. Each of his meals is catered to him, and he has a plush bed to carry him off to sleep each night. He wants for nothing and depends on no one. So when he is told there is something money cannot buy, it's a shock to his soul. The message that he is utterly dependent on the grace of God for salvation is a foreign concept to him. It's hard for him to wrap his mind around it.

Spiritually speaking, we all struggle to hear and understand the Gospel message. We all are inclined to reject it (Romans 1:28-32). Even the beggar would rather provide for himself than always rely on another. Inherent in our sinful nature is a desire to work for our salvation. We want to earn at least a part of it. The Bible is clear, however, that we cannot earn it. We are not justified before God by our good works (Galatians 2:16). If we could earn our way to Heaven by being good enough, then the cross of Christ would be pointless (Galatians 2:21).

This is why Jesus says that getting to Heaven on our own efforts is as impossible as fitting a camel through the eye of a needle. There is speculation among scholars that Jesus could have been talking about a certain gain leading into the city that was referred to as the eye of the needle. Those scholars go on to teach that the only way a camel could fit through that gate was by unloading anything it was carrying. Otherwise, it would be too big to fit. While that is a beautiful picture of the issue of the young man, it does not line up with Jesus' ultimate teaching on the situation.

Jesus answers the all too important question, "Then who can be saved?" with a striking answer. On our own, it is impossible. This takes the picture of the camel going through a gate and destroys it. A camel, indeed, could make it through a gate on its own. With help from friends or just sheer willpower, it could force its way through. The same is not true with our entrance into Heaven. According to Jesus, there is absolutely nothing we can do to save ourselves. It is impossible.

This is a hard pill to swallow because we are hard-wired to earn and perform. Every single religion in the world has a works-based system within it. If you do enough good things to outweigh the bad, then you'll be saved, reincarnated, etc. Christianity does not deny the importance of good works. Christians are told to be holy as God is holy (1 Peter 1:15-16). Where Christianity holds a stark contrast to the teachings of most other religions is that it doesn't require good works as a basis for our salvation.

It is impossible for man to save himself, but with God, all things are possible. This means that the only way anyone can be saved is if God intervenes. If we lack the goodness necessary to enter into His presence in Heaven, then we need God-level goodness attributed to us. How could that possibly happen? What could be done to remove the stain of sin and present us with garments of white?

THE IMPOSSIBLE MADE POSSIBLE

That is why his faith was "counted to him as righteousness." But the words "it was counted to him" were not written for his sake alone, but for ours also. It will be counted to us who believe in him who raised from the dead Jesus our Lord, who was delivered up for our trespasses and raised for our justification.

Romans 4:22-25

The incredible message of the Gospel of Jesus Christ is explained in the Book of Romans. Paul reaches all the way back to Genesis as he explains how men like Abraham were saved and granted entrance into Heaven. When Abraham heard the promises of God, he had faith. That faith was counted to him as righteousness (Genesis 15:6). In other words, because He believed in the promise of God, he was given a righteous standing before God.

Imagine having a bank account that showed a negative balance. You owed an impossible debt to the bank, and there was no way you would be able to pay it back. It's just a matter of time before the punishment for this negligence is brought down on you. Now imagine that someone goes to the bank on your behalf and puts that debt in their own name. This same person creates for you a new account and gives you an amount of funds that would be impossible to spend in a lifetime. This is what Jesus has done for all who believe. He took on the debt of sin and paid for it on the cross. He gives every believer a new standing before God, one that would mirror His own account of righteousness.

Paul boldly says in Romans that this is not only true of Abraham but for us as well. If we place our faith in Jesus, then His righteousness is credited to our account, while our sinfulness is born on the cross. As many have called it throughout the years, it was the great exchange: our sin for His perfection. The impossibility of an invitation to Heaven was removed when the Creator of Heaven and Earth died for sinful men like me and you.

On Earth As It Is In Heaven

We do not deserve a place in Heaven. We cannot have earned a seat at the heavenly banquet. And yet, by the grace of God, that is exactly what all Christians receive. It is truly an unbelievable gift. The more we realize the greatness of the gift of Heaven, the more it will impact our lives on Earth.

Just like Heaven will be, each day that we live on Earth is a gift from God (Ecclesiastes

3:2, 11). Although we may recognize this theologically, we don't often live like it is true. What would change in our daily routines if we were to focus on this each day? I believe that the coffee we drink would taste stronger. The flowers would smell sweeter. The moments we share with our families would give us deeper satisfaction and joy. All of life is enhanced when we realize that all of life is a gift.

It would serve our souls well if we were to take time to meditate on this truth each day. One of the best ways you can do this is by beginning each day with a time of prayer. In that time of speaking to God, you can confess to Him your daily need of Him. Jesus followed a pattern of morning prayer in His life and ministry (Mark 1:35). Because these prayers were done in private, we don't have a record of what exactly He prayed. However, we can be confident that they were prayers of His commitment to the will of the Father. Publically, He would tell His followers that He would do nothing apart from the Father (John 5:19).

Take time now to make plans to put this into practice. What time of day can you commit to praying to the Lord? Even if it is not in the morning, a set time of prayer would help you be consistent. After deciding when you can regularly pray, think about what you can pray about. Your mind will be drawn towards people who need help physically, but remember the eternal in your prayer life. What can you pray about that will affect your eternity? Who can you pray for for the sake of their eternity? If these kinds of prayers are regular things in our lives, then thinking of Heaven will be a daily occurrence. That kind of rhythm can change our whole outlook on life.

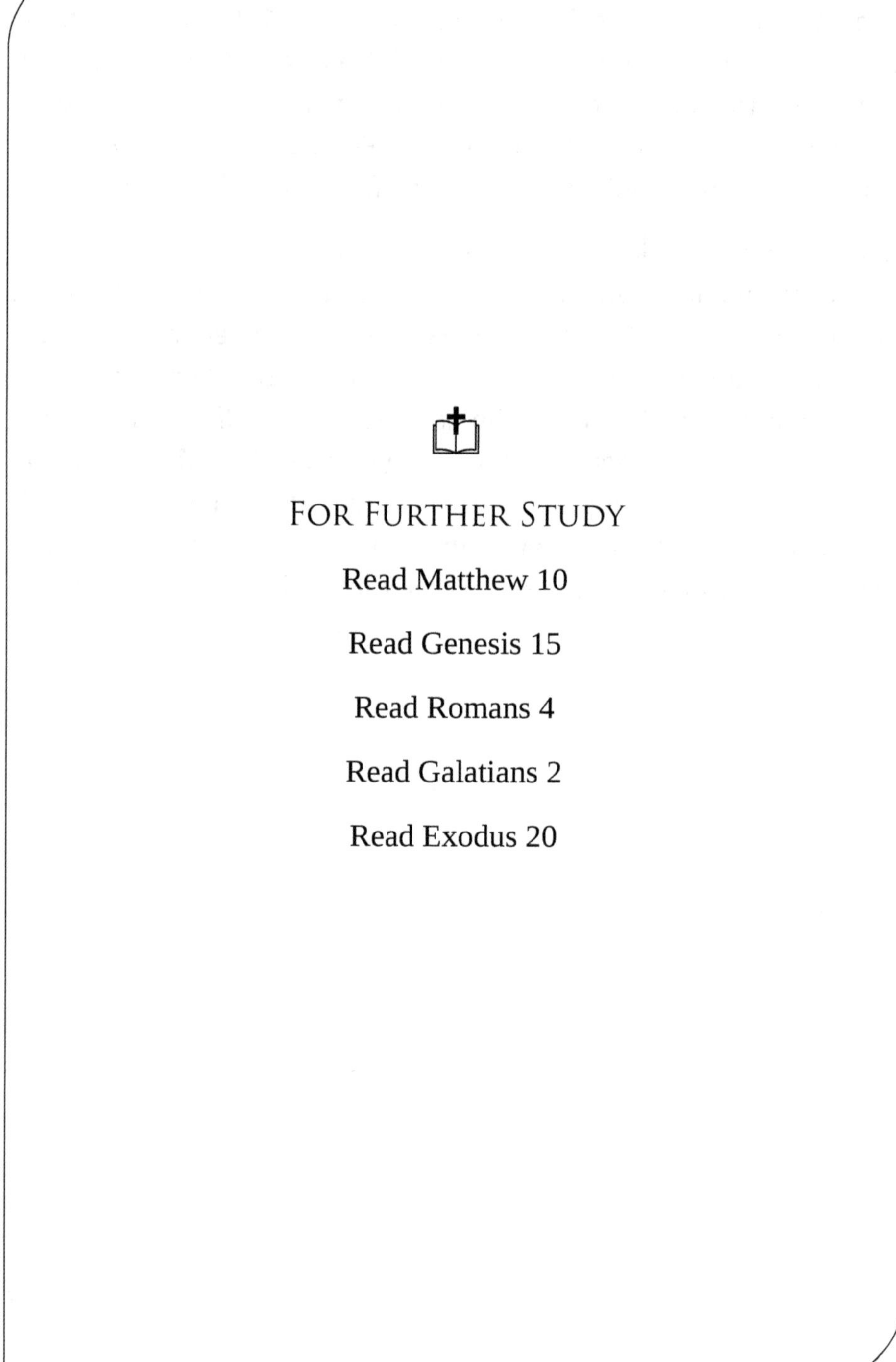

For Further Study

Read Matthew 10

Read Genesis 15

Read Romans 4

Read Galatians 2

Read Exodus 20

DISCUSSION QUESTIONS

1. Do you think the young man really thought he had kept the Law perfectly?

2. What would keep you from selling all you had to follow Jesus?

3. What is the hardest thing Jesus could ask you to give up Him?

4. Do you agree that there is no one who is good except for God? Why or why not?

5. Why do you think it is harder for the rich to see their need for God?

6. What challenges do the poor face in understanding their need for God?

7. How can you appreciate the gift of life today?

CHAPTER 3

LESS THAN HEAVEN

Heaven is a topic that has captivated the imagination of the world ever since the beginning. From theological books to cartoon comic strips, everyone seems to have weighed in on the subject. Some depictions of Heaven or heavenly things have become so commonplace in our culture that many have become confused. Because we see images and watch videos with these heavenly depictions, we may be convinced that what we see on the screen is what is described in the Bible. However, the majority of what has been created for entertainment purposes is less than Heaven.

Sure, they may contain some heavenly ideas, but they fall short of the glory that is described in the Bible. To be fair, very few of these authors, directors, and artists are claiming to give us an accurate depiction of our eternal home. But because these images have become so commonplace, it's important for us to point out what is not quite right about them.

CLOUDY PARADISE

In my experience, the most common depiction of Heaven on television or the movie screen is a cloudy paradise. The people that are shown walking around are essentially floating on a cloud. It looks a lot like we would if we were to walk down the street when it is very foggy outside. The white mist fades the background, and the focus is on the individuals traveling around. Occasionally, there will be added depictions of a golden gate or even God Himself in a three-piece suit. Whatever artistic details are added, the same cloudy paradise remains in most examples.

One of the primary reasons for this is that the original Hebrew and Greek words for heaven (the languages the Bible was first written in) are translated as "sky." Inherent in the very word is the thought of looking up to the sky. And when you do that, you will often find a cloud-filled sky. As people have looked up, imagining Heaven, it makes sense that their imagination takes our ceiling and makes it the floor of Heaven.

Although there is reasonable logic involved in the depiction of the cloudy paradise, it ignores entirely what the Bible says of Heaven. There is not one description of heaven that includes clouds or fog. In fact, one of the main descriptions of Heaven requires crystal clear vision as God will be the Light for all of eternity (Rev. 21:23). Will there be clouds? Perhaps. Will it be like we live in them? We have no biblical reason to think so.

MUSICAL ANGEL BABIES

One image of Heaven that has always confused me is one of musical angel babies. What has been drawn and painted for centuries are chubby, winged babies playing harps among the clouds. This type of artistic rendering began in the 14th century. The goal of these paintings was to display what a cherub would look like.

Once again, if you go back to the original languages of the Bible, this title for a type of angel can be literally translated to mean "child-like." The thought of the artist's ways to make a picture of a child-like angel. And thus were born the cute, chunky, diapered angels that occupy the cloudy paradise we have already discussed.

Sadly, this idea of what angels in Heaven would look like has no foundations in Scripture whatsoever. The first time a cherub is mentioned in the Bible, it is not lazily playing a musical instrument. It is standing at the gates to the Garden of Eden dawning a flaming sword and refusing entrance to Adam and Even. This passage doesn't give a description of the angelic body, but it would be hard to imagine this was the assignment of babies in the kingdom of God.

Furthermore, we are given a direct description of cherubim later in the Bible. Ezekiel, a prophet of God blessed with visions of the angels, describes the cherubim as creatures containing four faces of four creatures, only one of a human (Ezekiel 10:14). These cherubs are regularly seen in the Temple and Tabernacle, for God had the walls and the Ark of the Covenant designed with cherubim as the decorations. These cherubim are depicted as massive winged creatures that convey the distance between God and man ever since the Fall of Adam (1 Kings 6:24-25). The view of the heavenly hosts being musical angel babies is simply less than what is true.

Angelic Graduation

Another commonly held belief about the life to come is that when our loved ones die, they join the angels in Heaven. This angelic graduation has brought comfort to grieving families and has been marketed by all kinds of companies. You can buy greeting cards, ornaments, and paintings, all depicting a family member bearing angel wings. I was not able to find the origins of this belief, but it is clearly not found in the Bible.

We are currently considered lower than the angels, like our Savior when He was born on Earth (Hebrews 2:9). But this will not always be the case. Paul, when speaking about the great resurrection to come and the final judgment to follow, says that we will judge the angels (1 Corinthians 6:3), putting us above them as we reign with Christ. Angels long to look on and understand the Gospel that has granted us entrance into Heaven (1 Peter 1:12). This could not be true if angels were just formerly human. While we will be like angels in some respects (Luke 20:36), we will retain our humanity and be grateful for it in the end.

On Earth As It Is In Heaven

Having a view of Heaven that is too low will cause us to exalt earth too highly. If Heaven were an existence among the clouds where we become angels and play harps with our baby kindred, who among us would call that paradise? That eternity would feel more like an unusual, if not cruel, punishment. If that is what awaits the believer for all of eternity, we would be more drawn to stay here for as long as possible.

That cannot be what drove Paul to say, "to live is Christ and to die is gain" (Philippians 1:21). Surely that is not the joy that is in the presence of God (Psalm 16:11). Having a proper view of what Heaven will truly be like will increase our longing for it. It is important for us to know what the Bible says so that we can combat these false ideas that flood the media. We do not have to be belligerent when we see false depictions of eternity, but we must not accept them as fact.

For Further Study

Read Ezekiel 1

Read Ezekiel 10

Read 1 Kings 6

Read Exodus 36

Read Hebrews 2

Read 1 Corinthians 6

DISCUSSION QUESTIONS

1. What pictures of Heaven have you seen in our culture?'

2. What false ideas of Heaven did you have before?

3. How should you respond to a wrong view of Heaven?

4. How can you get a better understanding of what Heaven will be like?

5. In what ways will having a better understanding help you long for Heaven?

6. How will a greater view of Heaven change the way you live today?

7. Who can you help grow in their understanding of the biblical view of Heaven?

CHAPTER 4

HEAVEN'S HISTORY

The Christian Church has had disagreements over theology ever since the beginning. You can read of disagreements that Paul addressed in Galatians and that John addressed in 1 John. While there wasn't an addressed disagreement on Heaven recorded in the New Testament, there are different teachings that have come over the course of time. All of these teachings claim to be Christian teachings rooted in Scripture.

I'll explain each of them in this chapter, but let me begin with a disclaimer. I do not believe that any of these teachings are completely faithful to Scripture. Like in the last chapter, all of these have concepts that make them less than what Heaven is described as in the Bible.

The Christian Church has split into various factions over the course of its history based on theological positions. There are three very broad categories in which to think about the Christian Church. There is the Roman Catholic Church, Eastern Orthodox Church, and the Protestant Church. All three claim to hold to the most faithful representation of the Scriptures. As a member of the Protestant Church, I hold to that position as well. I will attempt to defend that as we examine the views of the Eastern Orthodox Church at present and the Roman Catholic Church later in this chapter.

EASTERN ORTHODOX - STATE OF BEING

The Eastern Orthodox Church teaches that Heaven is not a physical or spiritual place where people exist. It essentially teaches that Heaven is a state of being after death.

"[St Gregory of Nyssa] teaches that Paradise and Hell do not exist from God's point of view, but from man's point of view. It is a subject of man's choice and condition."

From God's perspective, according to the Eastern Orthodox Church, there is no Heaven or Hell. There is only the presence of God everywhere. So when we die, our souls are fully enveloped in the presence of God. That sounds like Heaven, right? Well, the teaching continues to say that from our perspective, those who die without salvation will be blinded to the presence of God. That state of being, the feeling of being cut off from God, will be Hell. Conversely, those who die with salvation will be fully aware of the presence of God. That state of being will be Heaven.

Without any doubt, God is omnipresent. The Bible is clear is Psalm 139, where the psalmist says, "Where shall I go from your Spirit? Or where shall I flee from your presence? If I ascend to heaven, you are there! If I make my bed in Sheol, you are there!" No matter where you are physically, God is there. But God has not manifested His presence everywhere. In the glory and majesty of our God, He can be everywhere and be manifested in a singular location at the same time.

Moses was blessed to have one of these experiences in Exodus 33. In the tent of meeting, he met with God ``face to face" (Exodus 33:11). At this moment, when the glory of the Lord was made manifest before Moses, God did not give up His presence outside of the tent of meeting. He was at the same time present at all places and manifestly present in the tent of the meeting.

With this in mind, let's consider the Eastern Orthodox teaching of Heaven and Hell as a state of being that either has or does not have an awareness of God's presence. We can heartily agree on this main premise: the essence of Heaven and Hell is the presence of God. In Heaven, we will fully know and be known by God. His presence, unhindered by our sin, will be a blissful existence. On the other hand, Hell is the devastating loss of the presence of God. Anyone in Hell will be painfully aware that God is not there.

The question at hand is, "Is that experience truly a matter of time and space, or is it a matter of being and awareness?" The overall teaching of the Bible is that Heaven and Hell are actual places. They are given physical descriptions with relative boundaries. There are distinct rewards and punishments given to the sheep and goats in Matthew 25. These rewards and punishments are described as the kingdom of God and the eternal fire. In Revelation 21, the final home of all people will either be on the New Earth in New Jerusalem that has boundary markers described (Revelation 21:15-17) or the lake of fire (Revelation 20:14-15). None of the descriptions given would naturally lead to an experience described by the Eastern Orthodox Church.

One of the best examples of this comes from Jesus' teachings on Heaven and Hell, found in a parable in Luke 16:19-31.

The poor man died and was carried by the angels to Abraham's side. The rich man also died and was buried, and in Hades, being in torment, he lifted up his eyes and saw Abraham far off and Lazarus at his side.

Luke 16:22-23, ESV

There is a lot to be gleaned from this parable, but for our purposes now, take note of the awareness of each person's location. For both Lazarus and the poor man, it says that they were in a new location after their death. Both were buried, and both spiritually awoke in a new place. For the poor man, it was on Abraham's side, which is another name for Heaven. And for Lazarus, it was in Hades, which is another name for Hell. If Heaven were merely a state of being, then Jesus would have no reason to use travel language. And yet He expressly says that the soul of the poor man is carried away by angels.

Furthermore, the two men in the parable are clearly aware of their own state and the state of the other person. Later on in the parable, they communicate with one another and are very aware of each other's situation

(Luke 16:24). It would not make sense for them to be aware of one another but unaware of the God who put them in those locations.

Finally, Lazarus makes an impassioned plea for someone to return to his family and save them from his plight (Luke 16:27). Once again, this uses language that assumes a change in location and not just a change in a state of being. The eastern orthodox position simply does not align fully with Scripture. We can appreciate their understanding of the spiritual state. But we cannot deny the specific locations that scripture shows us.

ROMAN CATHOLICISM - PURGATORY

The Roman Catholic Church differs greatly from the Protestant Church on many points of theology. The separation between them is so great that the moment they split is referred to as "The Reformation." Men like Martin Luther, Ulrich Zwingli, John Calvin, and many others led the charge to separate from the Roman Catholic Church.

One of the things they differed on was the concept of "purgatory." This word is not found in the Bible, but Roman Catholics insist that the concept is clearly there. Purgatory is one of three places the soul may go after death. At this point, you're familiar with Heaven and Hell, but Purgatory may be a new idea. Let me explain in simple terms. Purgatory is a place where a soul may still be cleansed from sin. If someone goes to the spiritual holding room of Purgatory, they may still end up in Heaven.

The Roman Catholic Church taught this idea using a few Scriptures as their basis. The first is found in Matthew 12, where it says,

And whoever speaks a word against the Son of Man will be forgiven, but whoever speaks against the Holy Spirit will not be forgiven, either in this age or in the age to come.

Matthew 12:32, ESV

This statement is made in the midst of a larger conversation on the "un-pardonable sin" of blasphemy against the Holy Spirit. The way Roman Catholics teach about Purgatory from this passage is by pointing out the forgiveness that is not offered "in this age or in the age to come." They say that this verse implies that forgiveness can be given or denied in our present life and in our life to come.

There are two issues with this interpretation of this passage. The first issue with that interpretation of the passage lies in what is meant by "the age to come." It most likely refers to life after death, but it must at least be questioned. In two different places in the New Testament, "ages" to come are addressed (1 Corinthians 10:11, Ephesians 2:7). Who is to say which age we are in and how many more ages there are to come before the final age of eternal life (Mark 10:30)?

The second is that the passage only explicitly confirms that a lack of forgiveness may come in this age and the age to come. Forgiveness is only clearly offered in this current age. It is a huge assumption to say that there is implicit forgiveness in the age to come. If this were the case, Jesus could have easily added that into the first part of the statement. It is definitely not a clear teaching on forgiveness to come after death, although it could be argued. If this passage alone was the basis for the teaching of purgatory, then it would be quickly denied by all Christen-dom. However, this is another passage that they turn to to prove their point.

If anyone's work is burned up, he will suffer loss, though he him-self will be saved, but only through fire.

1 Corinthians 3:15, ESV

This passage of Scripture comes in the context of a larger discussion of the Day of the Lord. It is taught in this passage that on that Day, God will put the good works of the believers to the test. Some works will be burned up like wood, hay, or straw (1 Corinthians 3:12). Others will stand the test of fire, like gold, silver, or precious stones. All will be put through the fire, and only what is good will remain (1 Corinthians 3:13).

After Paul makes these analogies, he ends with the verse quoted above. The Roman Catholic Church would teach that the process of going through the fire, suffering loss, and then being saved in the end is indicative of Purgatory. That is the essential point of Purgatory. A soul that still remains unclean can be purified before ultimately being saved and granted entrance into Heaven.

The issue with this interpretation is two-fold. The first is that life after death isn't the topic at hand. The judgment of the works of the believer is the focus. To make an interpretative point about a destination for the soul after death would have to be a stretch.

Secondly, that interpretation misses the significance of verse 11, which says, "For no one can lay a foundation other than that which is laid, which is Jesus Christ." In these verses, the foundation of everyone being judged is Jesus Christ. What is being burned is anything that is laid on top of that foundation. This means that the only judgment being described in 1 Corinthians 3 is the judgment regarding the good works of believers.

According to Paul, it may be that all is burned up. But that individual would still be saved in the end, not because of one precious stone or ounce of gold, but because of the foundation they built on. Faith in Jesus saves anyone who has it, regardless of the mansion of good works they may build upon it.

The fundamental issue with the Roman Catholic teaching on Purgatory is that it devalues what Jesus accomplished for His people on the cross. According to the Bible, when a person places their faith in Jesus, their eternity is secured. They are made at peace with God (Romans 5:2). Believers have their record of wrong wiped clean at the moment of faith (1 Corinthians 6:11). Paul makes it clear that we add nothing to our salvation aside from the sin that was made necessary in Ephesians 2.

There it says,

> *But God, being rich in mercy, because of the great love with which he loved us, even when we were dead in our trespasses, made us alive together with Christ—by grace you have been saved . . . And this is not your own doing; it is the gift of God, not a result of works, so that no one may boast.*
>
> ***Ephesians 2:4-5; 8b-9, ESV***

Just as dead men cannot raise themselves back to life, we cannot save ourselves. God, in His unchanging love, raised us back to life by grace through faith in His Son. Paul furthers this point by saying that our salvation is not of our own works so that no man may boast. If this is true, then there is simply no need for a Purgatory state.

The clear teaching of the Bible is that once you place your faith in Jesus, your eternal home is switched from a rightful punishment in Hell to a graciously given home in Heaven. There is no in-between. Paul wrote in another part of Scripture that for the believer, "to be absent from the body is to be present with the Lord" (2 Corinthians 5:8). There is no holding room for the soul.

Jehovah's Witness - 144,000 Anointed

These final two views of eternity come from groups that claim the name Christianity, but they are not widely accepted by the three main branches of Christianity that have already been mentioned. Their views are worth considering, but please understand that these would be views not widely held by people who claim to be Christians.

The first of the final two that we will consider comes from a group known as Jehovah's Witnesses. They teach a concept that essentially says that Heaven has a limited capacity. There will be only 144,000 people who will be granted a seat there while the rest of the believers will remain on Earth. They get this idea from the final book of the Bible.

As you have probably already pointed out in your own mind, if this passage is to be taken literally, it poses a problem for many members of the Jehovah's Witness faith. This passage seems to be saying that a limited number of nationally Jewish people will be saved in a special way. Therefore, if your lineage doesn't reach back to the original tribes of Israel, then this cannot apply to you.

It would be hard to hold too tightly to a literal interpretation of this passage of Scripture, however. The number 12 is significant all the way throughout the Bible. There are 12 tribes of Israel. There are 12 disciples chosen by Jesus. There are 12 apostles in the church. These 12's are represented in the walls of the New Jerusalem (Revelation 21:14).

Since much of Revelation is analogous to other things, it is likely that the author is using the important numbers in the Bible to make a bigger point. The point could be that the 12 represents a completeness to God's people. It may very well be that Revelation 7 describes a full restoration of God's original people, the nation of Israel.

Even this interpretation brings unique challenges to anyone of the Jehovah's Witness faith to claim a spot among the 144,000. Therefore, they take the whole passage in a spiritual sense and say that Israel is synonymous with any believer. They would contend that there is a special class of believers who would experience this kind of grace in being chosen as a part of the 144,000.

This issue with treating this passage as completely a spiritual analogy is that believers, in general, are mentioned specifically later on in Revelation 7.

After this I looked, and behold, a great multitude that no one could number, from every nation, from all tribes and peoples and languages, standing before the throne and before the Lamb, clothed in white robes, with palm branches in their hands, and crying out with a loud voice, "Salvation belongs to our God who sits on the throne, and to the Lamb!"

Revelation 7:9-10, ESV

If Revelation 7:4-8 is a spiritual representation of any believer who meets the special, unknown qualifications for being a part of the 144,000, then who does the multitude represent? In the multitude, there are believers from every nation, tribe, and language. You have to jump through a lot of hoops and offer a lot of unreasonable explanations to maintain that this passage of Scripture is only to be taken in an analogous way.

Finally, in all of Revelation 7, there is no clear teaching that there is a special place or reign for the 144,000. Whoever they are, from whatever nation they may hail from, there is no explicit text that says they will reign in Heaven while the remaining believers will stay on earth. In fact, the New Earth in New Jerusalem is said to be the place where God's people will reign (Revelation 22:5).

MORMONISM - DEGREES OF GLORY

Mormonism, more formally known as The Church of Jesus Christ of the Latter-Day Saints, is the final view of Heaven that we will consider in this chapter. As I mentioned before, this group claims to be a Christian group but would not be widely affirmed by the Roman Catholic Church, Eastern Orthodox Church, or the Protestant Church.

In the teaching of Mormonism, every believer will be raised in a great resurrection in a physically glorified body (1 Thessalonians 4:16). They believe that our souls go into a rest-state until that day. It would be a purgatory-like holding place without the chance of cleansing. We have already addressed that idea at length, so we will skip it in this section.

In the great resurrection to come, it is taught that believers will be placed into one of three levels of glory or Heaven. There is the celestial kingdom (the highest glory), the terrestrial kingdom (the middle glory), and the telestial kingdom (the lowest glory). Finally, there is a version of Hell that exists in Mormon theology. It is one of the annihilation of the unbeliever. These levels of glory are based on a passage found in 1 Corinthians 15, which says,

There are heavenly bodies and earthly bodies, but the glory of the heavenly is of one kind, and the glory of the earthly is of another. There is one glory of the sun, and another glory of the moon, and another glory of the stars; for star differs from star in glory.

1 Corinthians 15:40-41, ESV

Did you notice the three levels of glory that Paul mentions in his letter to the church in Corinth? He says there are three glories. One is found in the son, the next in the moon, and finally in the stars. The teaching of the Mormon church is that these three levels (son, moon, and stars) are representative of the three levels of glory to come (celestial, terrestrial, and telestial).

The highest of these kingdoms is the celestial kingdom. This would be the place where God the Father and Jesus dwell. When we think of Heaven, this would be the location that we think of. This celestial kingdom is reserved for those who not only believe but have shown excellency in their good works and furtherance of the message of Joseph Smith (the founder of the Church of Jesus Christ of the Latter Day Saints).

The following two degrees of glory are a little more difficult to understand. The terrestrial kingdom, the middle level of glory, is reserved for those who live a good life but did not fully commit to the Gospel of Jesus Christ, according to Mormonism. I question whether or not there would be any glory for those who did not follow Jesus whole-heartedly (Matthew 16:24), but we can debate that in another section. For now, we will take the point of the Mormon teaching that there is a second level of glory based on the goodness of the believer.

Finally, there is the lowest level of glory that is comparable to the glory of the stars. It is the telestial kingdom. This kingdom is reserved for those who lived selfish lives and rejected God altogether. The only reason they have been granted entrance into the kingdom was because God expressed His love towards them and saved them anyways.

There are all kinds of issues with this teaching on Heaven from Mormonism. Let's begin with the performance-based placement in Heaven. The Bible clearly teaches that there will be rewards for believers based on their good works (Matthew 5:12; Luke 6:23, 35; 1 Corinthians 3:14; 9:18). However, this is a teaching for true believers only. Those who merely do good works without a full commitment to the Gospel will be cast away (Matthew 7:21-23). Those who openly reject God and live apart from Him stand no chance of salvation and a place in Heaven (Matthew 10:33). The entire system of salvation and reward for anyone who does not place their faith in Jesus and receive the grace of God (Ephesians 2:8) is foreign to the Bible.

The second major issue with this understanding of 1 Corinthians 15 is that Paul is not discussing levels of Heaven's glory. His point is much simpler when you consider the context of what he is teaching. He is simply stating that in the resurrection, there will be a difference in the bodies our souls occupy. The bodies we have now are earthly. The bodies we will have in heaven are heavenly. They have differing levels of glory. Paul goes on to explain the difference of glory in the following verses, which state,

To take this passage of Scripture and use is to prove a theory about Heaven itself is an improper use of the text. While it is discussing heavenly things, the subject of Heaven is not the focus. The Mormon interpretation of this passage of Scripture is simply wrong. But the Mormons do not limit themselves to the Bible for their understanding of eternity. They also refer highly, if not more often, to the Book of Mormon. There may be plenty of justification for such teaching in this book, but that will not be discussed in this book. As a Christian book for true Christians, the Bible is the only sacred text we will consider.

ON EARTH AS IT IS IN HEAVEN

Without any debate, the Bible does not answer every question about Heaven. There are a lot of things that are left for our wonder and speculation. However, the Bible does make plain the most important items regarding Heaven. The core things that every believer needs to know are found within its pages.

The Bible is clear that only those who place their faith in Jesus and receive the grace of God will be granted entrance to Heaven. It plainly teaches that there are rewards for believers in Heaven, but the rewards are not various positions in various kingdoms. The most natural reading of the Bible declares Heaven to be an actual place for the believer and not just a state of being. And while there may be a literal 144,000 that have a special place in the heart of God in Heaven, it would be a poor understanding of Revelation 7 to think that those people come from anywhere aside from the nation of Israel.

If we are going to pray and hope for God to make His will on Earth as it is in Heaven, then we must take the Bible at its Word. We may have ideas, speculation, and wondrous thoughts about the things of God. But if they are not supported by the Bible, we must be hesitant to hold them in a theological position. At the end of the day, it's possible that heaven is a state of being or that there are levels of glory. But the Bible does not explicitly teach those things. In some cases, the Bible is clearly against those ideas. If there is any doubt in what the Bible is saying, we must pull back to what is clear. The rest must be held loosely. And some of our ideas need to be dropped altogether. There are clear warnings in the Old and New Testaments about adding or taking away from God's Word (Deuteronomy 4:2, Revelation 22:19).

With the warning in Revelation, there is a punishment described if we do alter or add to the Word of God with our man-made ideas. The consequence of such an action is that "God will take away his share in the tree of life and in the holy city, which are described in this book." This is not teaching that God will remove the salvation of a believer based on his actions. What we have not earned, we cannot lose (John 10:28). What it is teaching is that anyone who would willingly alter or add to the Word of God is not a true believer. In this holy book, we have all we need for life and godliness (2 Peter 1:3). To alter or add to God's Word is to call into question all of Scripture and the mind of God by saying that it is not enough. God lied. There must be more truth to behold. That is a dangerous position to hold.

For Further Study

Read Deuteronomy 4:1-8

Read Revelation 22

Read 1 Corinthians 15:35-49

Read Revelation 7

Read 1 Corinthians 3:10-23

DISCUSSION QUESTIONS

1. Were any of the views of Heaven mentioned in this chapter new to you?

2. Which of these views would you be most likely to believe?

3. What still needs explanation for you?

4. Why is it more likely that Heaven is a place and not a state of being?

5. Can someone enter into Heaven without faith? Why or why not?

6. What kind of rewards can we expect in Heaven?

7. What can you do to solidify in your mind what the Bible teaches about Heaven?

Chapter 5

The Dwelling Place of God

Now that we have done the hard work of determining what is not true about heaven, we can begin the wonderful process of figuring out what heaven is like. We will look at both the Old and the New Testament for our answers. But for now, we will settle in the Old Testament and see that the primary picture presented is that heaven is the dwelling place of God.

The very first use of the word "heaven" found in Scripture needs some serious explanation. The Hebrew word translated into heaven literally means "sky." The first use of the word says that there are multiple heavens. You know this verse better than you think because it is the very first verse of your Bible. "In the beginning, God created the heavens and the earth" (Genesis 1:1). Many verses contain the word "heavens" instead of the singular "heaven." Below are just a few:

"The heavens declare the glory of God, and the sky above proclaims his handiwork."

Psalm 19:1, ESV.

"But who is able to build him a house, seeing the heaven and heaven of heavens cannot contain him? Who am I then, that I should build him a house, save only to burn sacrifice before him?"

2 Chronicles 2:6, ESV

What's going on here? Are there multiple dwelling places of God? Is there more than one heaven? What did Moses mean when he wrote that God made the heavens in the beginning? Scripturally, there are three "heavens" or three "skies" that are referred to in Scripture. There is the sky as we know it, our atmosphere. There is Outer Space, the second layer of the heavens. Finally, there is Heaven, as we think of it, standing as the third and final layer of the heavens. We find scriptural justification for this in the letter Paul wrote to the church in Corinth.

Paul recalls a time when he was speaking with someone who had seen a vision of heaven. Although there are some details that Paul is not sure of in regard to the encounter, there is one thing he makes plain: that this man was brought to the third heaven. There is no reason to think that this is one of three different heavens where God dwells. But this is simply the third layer, the highest point, the true Heaven that we normally think of when we hear the word.

There is a reason that when people think of God in heaven, they point up and look up: the very word directs their gaze to the sky. As you read your Bible and you come across the words "heaven" and "heavens," pay attention to the context, and you'll be able to determine pretty easily what the author means. For our purposes in this book, we are going to settle on a few passages that explicitly say "heaven" or imply the highest Heaven, God's dwelling place.

Throughout the Old Testament, Heaven is considered to be the dwelling place of God. This incredible truth is celebrated in the Book of Psalms. I was amazed as I worked my way through the Bible to see how often "heaven" or "heavens" is used in the songs of God's people. It makes me think maybe we ought to spend more time singing about our glorious home to come. As you go through the Psalms, there are two ideas that are foundational to Heaven's reality. Both are found in Psalm 11:4.

The Lord is in his holy temple; the Lord's throne is in heaven; his eyes see, his eyelids test the children of man.

Psalm 11:4, ESV

THE DWELLING PLACE OF GOD

Do you need proof of the reality of Heaven? God Himself dwells there! It is where He has set His throne. It is His perfect domain, untarnished by sin. When God created the heavens and the earth, he made this round ball we live on, the atmosphere to make it viable, the space to hold it in place, and His own home.

The Bible clearly teaches that God is omnipresent (Psalm 139) and that God dwells in special ways among His people. He walked with Adam and Eve in the Garden (Genesis 2). He talked with Abraham on many occasions (Genesis 12). He revealed Himself to Moses through a burning bush and pillar of cloud (Exodus 3:2, 13:21). He dwelled in the Tabernacle and the Temple (Exodus 25:8).

But the idea more prominent than any of these in the Old Testament is that God's perfect dwelling is in Heaven. He was in and out of the Garden. He left the Temple. The bush that burned with His glory returned to its fashion. But Heaven has always been the home of God. It is there that His throne sits.

Heaven is the place of God's primary residence. If God's glory was known to be in the Holy of Holies in the midst of the Temple, then Heaven is like one giant Holy of Holies. There is no hiding or hindering his glory there. In a glorious array, he fills up the space. From his throne, he directs the actions of the angels. He casts judgment on the wicked. And he welcomes the redeemed sinner into his presence. It is in this perfect place that he watches over creation and intervenes when he desires.

And make no mistake, dear friend. God does intervene when he will. He has not set the world in motion and let it fend for itself. He has not kicked Adam and Eve out of the garden just so that they might die. He constantly interacts with his people through personal encounters, through the proclamation of his word, and most powerfully through the person of his son, Jesus Christ. As you continue reading Psalm 11, you will see that the throne room of God contains a window for him to peer out of before he springs into action.

HEAVEN'S WINDOW

Over and over again, the Psalms contain this idea that Heaven has a window (Psalm 14:2; 33:13; 53:2; 80:4; 85:11; 102:19). This implies one really important truth about Heaven. It is a distinct place. We're talking about Nirvana or this idea that we are absorbed into God as Heaven." It is a distinct place where God is, and we are not.

And from this distinct place, the Lord of all creation reigns. As he keeps his eye on the hands and hearts of men. He is able to distribute blessings and curses as is appropriate (Deuteronomy 28). The blessings and the curses are not a one-for-one correspondence. Each sin does not equal one curse. But God does respond to the nature of man to draw him to repentance. So, for the men who are living in sin, he will use various means to open their eyes. Sadly, there does come a point where he may give them over to their debased minds (Romans 1:24, 26, 28). Generally speaking, God works and speaks so that all men will come to know and follow him.

The window of Heaven is not just a place from which God can throw lightning bolts down to earth. It is a place from which he can peer into the hearts of men and seek to do them good. It is the place from which he raises dead men back to life. It is the place from which he works through the hands of prophets and apostles to heal the sick and the lame. Yes, judgment does come down from heaven, but so does mercy and grace.

Depending on your spiritual state, the thought of God, looking down from heaven on your life, may strike fear or comfort into your heart. If you have been saved by the gospel of Jesus Christ, then it is the greatest comfort to know that God is looking out over you. It is a wonderful thing to think that he has a plan for you (Jeremiah 29:11). It is a true joy to wonder at the eye that not only watches the sparrow but watches over you as well (Matthew 6:25-27).

But if you are not a believer in the gospel of Jesus Christ. Then, as God watches your life unfold, He will see every sin that comes forward. And each of those sins is worthy of eternal judgment, according to the Bible. So, the eye of God on you ought to strike more fear in your heart than you even realize. I hope that you'll open your eyes to the truth of what the Bible says and run to the forgiveness that only comes through faith in Jesus.

According to the Old Testament, Heaven is the true dwelling place of God. These ideas are repeated throughout the first half of the Bible. Jacob's ladder leads to Heaven (Genesis 28:10-17). Elijah was taken up to Heaven in a chariot of fire (2 Kings 2:11). It is there that Job knows His Redeemer lives (Job 19:25). But it is not that His Redeemer stays. The reality of Heaven and the God whom it holds changes our lives today.

The fact that there is a God who occupies heaven and reigns from his throne changes how we view ourselves. It puts our lives into proper perspective. Just think about it on a physical scale. How small we are in comparison to the world is nothing when you put it into comparison to God himself. The Creator of the vast world that we are just a blip of must surely be infinitely larger than us. So therefore, who are we to stand up against him? Who are we to go against his ways? Who are we to rebel against his rule?

When I think about this, it reminds me of a time when I joined my high school football team. Now, I am a relatively small person. And one of the exercises that our coaches had us do was to wrestle over a rope in practice. I was paired up against one of the largest and strongest men on the team. It is not an exaggeration to say that he slung me around like a ragdoll. I felt like I was in the midst of a tornado as I tried, just simply, to hold on for dear life. But the wrestling match was over. That person committed to being my friend. He had my back to speak for the rest of the season.

When I think about God and his people, this is what comes to mind. The true and honest answer to those questions before is that we are nothing, save what the Lord declares us to be. To the praise of his wonderful grace and name, he declares us to be of value and worth. The Bible says that we are made in his image. This means that we have intrinsic value and dignity because of what he has made us to be. So, if we owe all of our value and worth to the one who has created us, why would we not give him every ounce of that back?

Friend, I challenge you in light of who God is and from where he reigns to consider yourself rightly. You nor I are God. We do not have the right or the authority to call the shots. We do not get to decide what is right and what is wrong. We do not get to make decisions on how best to live life. All of these things belong to the creator. These are the decisions to be made by the king of kings and the Lord of lords. He is the only one who has that kind of wisdom and that kind of authority.

Perhaps one of the best ways for you and I to remember these truths is to simply look up. Each and every day, we ought to take a moment to look up to the skies and consider the heavens. The clouds display and declare the majesty of God. The sun is a reflection of the light that he is. The stars are a show of his brilliance. And so if we were to take time just to simply look up and let those things that we see be a reminder of who he is and the power that he has, we would be better for it.

If you are like me, when you see the sunset or the sunrise, it takes your breath away. It causes you to think and wonder at the one who could design such beauty. That is a good thing for us. It is a wonderful privilege for us to see and recognize the hand of God and creation. And yet, too often, our eyes are drawn to lesser things. Our phones and computers have overtaken our minds. We spend more time watching TV than enjoying the nature that God has created.

To be clear, phones, computers, and televisions are not bad things. They are gifts from God as well. But there is something different about considering creation. This is why the Bible says that the heavens declare the glory of God, as we read in Psalm 19. Spend time in nature. Look up. Take in the wonders of the thunderstorms and the beauty of the shooting stars. Let those things cast your mind and your affections on the God who created them and you.

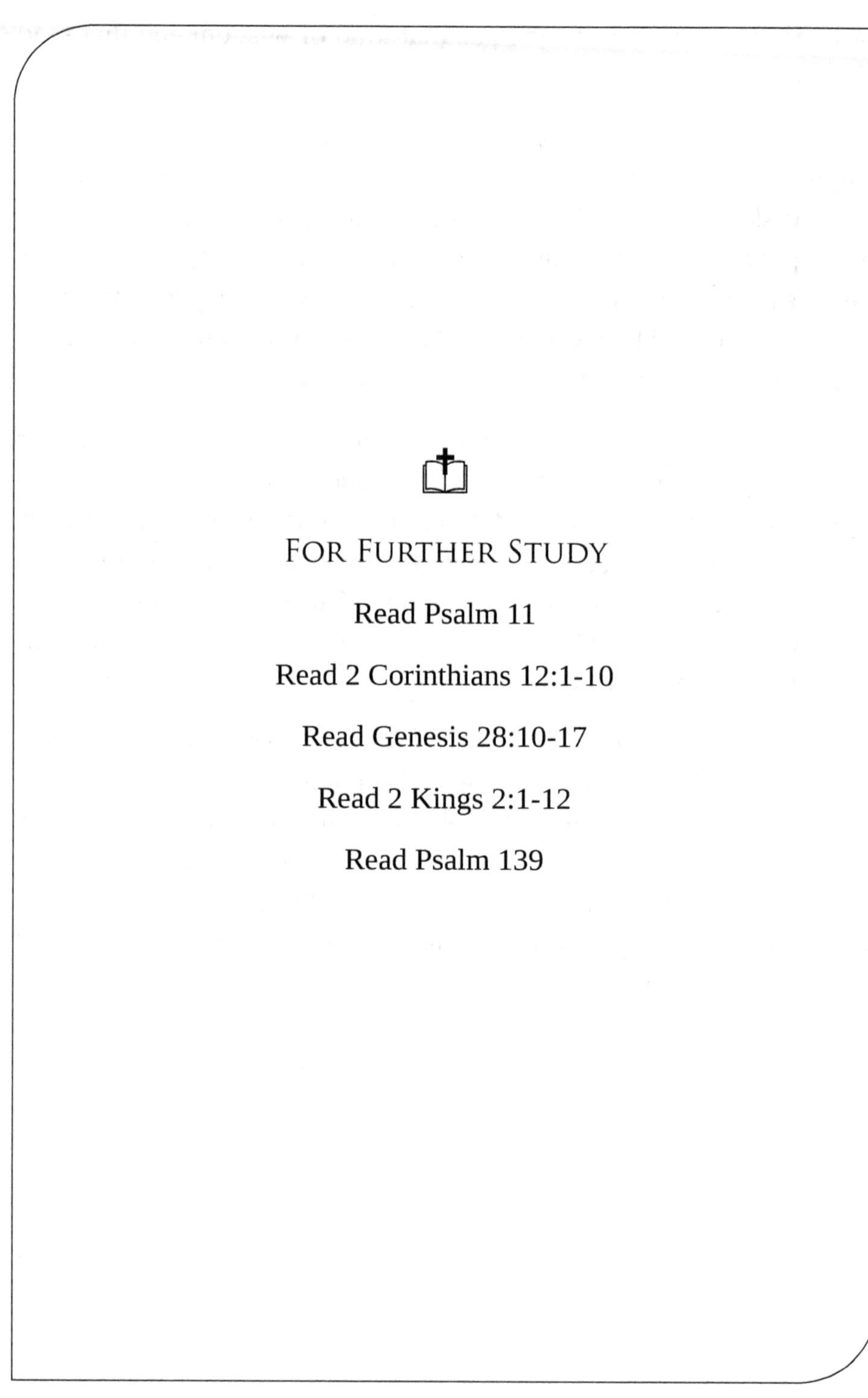

For Further Study

Read Psalm 11

Read 2 Corinthians 12:1-10

Read Genesis 28:10-17

Read 2 Kings 2:1-12

Read Psalm 139

1. What are the different heavens that God created in Genesis 1:1?

2. Why do people look to or point to the sky when talking about Heaven?

3. What does it mean for God to be looking at us from Heaven?

4. How does God's observance of your life make you feel?

5. Why is God's throne in Heaven and not on Earth?

6. Why do you think Heaven is primarily seen as God's dwelling place in the Old Testament?

7. What remains unsaid about Heaven in the Old Testament?

Chapter 6

The Home of the Believer

There is no place like home. It has a distinct smell. It brings you a sense of comfort that you cannot find anywhere else. I don't know about you, but I sleep the best when I am at home. Even the most luxurious of hotels can be compared to a good night's rest in the place you know and love. It is wonderful that heaven is described as our home. Jesus says that it is a place that is prepared for us.

I can remember when I first went off to college, I had committed to staying there for multiple months before returning home. I wanted to make sure that I got over the homesickness so that I could fully commit to the college experience. And so I waited for three or four months before going back home. But no matter how long I was away, the moment I walked through my old front door. It hit me. The overwhelming sense and feeling of comfort that comes with going home.

It is interesting to think about Heaven in this way. Because heaven is a place that we have never been. It is hard to imagine that a foreign place will feel like home when we arrive. And yet, this is the promise of scripture. There will be no place Day to our heart, then in the eternal rest of heaven.

Jesus spoke about Heaven and Hell often in his teaching ministry. He actually taught more about Hell than Heaven, but that's a topic for a later time. One of his most famous teachings on Heaven is indirect but still very clear.

"Let not your hearts be troubled. Believe in God; believe also in me. In my Father's house there are many rooms. If it were not so, would I have told you that I go to prepare a place for you? And if I go and prepare a place for you, I will come again and will take you to myself, that where I am you may be also. 4 And you know the way to where I am going."

John 14:1-3, ESV

HEAVEN IS A PREPARED PLACE

Wait a minute! I thought God had already created the heavens and the earth? What is He talking about? What is Jesus going to do? Hasn't that work already been done? Ultimately, there will be a new heaven and a new earth as described in Revelation (we'll discuss that in another chapter), but until then, there are "mansions" or better translated "rooms" prepared for those who die before Jesus' return.

Before this conversation began, Jesus said some pretty hard things to his disciples. In the 13th chapter of the book of John, Jesus makes two astonishing revelations. The first is that one of his disciples will betray him. We find out later that this disciple is Judas. Judas will Sell Jesus for a small amount of silver. This betrayal will lead to his crucifixion. This is no small thing for Jesus to insert into dinner conversation.

He also tells of the denial that Peter will bring. Three times. Peter is to deny Jesus. This is devastating news for this disciple. Peter denies that he will deny Jesus. But we see you later on in scripture that Peter does just this. Three times over, he denies knowing or having any association with Jesus.

And so it is no wonder that Jesus begins chapter 14 with the comforting words, "Let your hearts be troubled." Here, we learn that heaven is supposed to be a source of comfort for us. Our source of comfort that comes most assured in times of trial and persecution. When we feel like we are far from God because of the mistakes that we have made, we always remember that there is a place prepared for us.

It is hard for me to think about Jesus in this way. Someone who is going to serve us. My view of Him as Master and Lord. How can my Savior and King serve me? But the reality is that this is the kind of King He is. He is a servant leader through and through. His mission statement in the Gospel, according to Mark, states that "The Son of Man did not come to be served, but to serve and to give His life as a ransom for many" (Mark 10:45).

If you have ever spent the night at a friend's house and you know what kind of service this is. They make a bed for you. They provide hot meals for you. They do their best to make you feel at home. In a much greater sense, as Jesus goes to prepare a place for his people, he is preparing a home for them. Not just so they might feel at home but so they would actually be at home. Heaven is our home, according to the Bible. It is a place that is prepared for us.

HEAVEN IS A PLACE FOR FUTURE TREASURES

From these verses, we learn that Heaven is where Jesus came from, it's where the saints live with God, and it's the place where Jesus continues to work on our future heavenly home. There is no doubt in Jesus' mind that heaven is a reality. But if you're unsure because he used the phrase "my Father's house" instead of heaven, turn to another Gospel account. Matthew 6:19-21 says,

> *"Do not lay up for yourselves treasures on earth, where moth and rust destroy and where thieves break in and steal, but lay up for yourselves treasures in heaven, where neither moth nor rust destroys and where thieves do not break in and steal. For where your treasure is, there your heart will be also."*
>
> ***Matthew 6:19-21, ESV***

Here, Jesus could not be speaking of the other "heavens," like the sky or outer space. How ridiculous for Him to command us to ship our treasures into space where they'll be safe. The only thing He could mean is Heaven, as we think of it. What's interesting about these verses is that they teach that what we do on earth has an effect on our lives in heaven.

Our temporary physical life affects our eternal spiritual life. While Heaven is this place where God dwells and we do not, we are not disconnected from it. There are rooms prepared for His People and treasures to be stored there. The reality of Heaven is that you were in mind when it was created.

We can only offer speculation as to what these treasures may be. We are told of various crowns we can earn for good work. And we are told that we will have the crowd of life. All of these crowns will be laid at the feet of Jesus. We are not told explicitly what these treasures that we can store up may be.

Perhaps this means that we will have a seat closer to the savior at the table. Maybe this just simply means that we will have a more luxurious lifestyle in heaven. Whatever it may mean at the end of the day, it will mean very little to us when standing in the presence of God. Whatever home has been prepared for us with whatever treasures may be, there will be more than enough. We will see that it is all of Grace and that we deserve none of it. And so, even if we have a coat closet in heaven, it will be sufficient for our needs.

This realization is not to deter us from working hard to store treasures in heaven. But it is to help put everything into perspective. That the treasures here on earth really do not last very long. The treasures in heaven are going to be eternal. But even those will pale in comparison to the savior who has provided the treasure for us. Just like the crowns that the elders around the throne of God will cast before his feet, we two will willingly submit all of our treasures to the use of the savior.

And so the question rifle comes next. How do you store up treasures in heaven? What kind of work accomplishes that goal. As far as I know, there are no bank accounts that we can set up now that will be valid in the heavenly realm. So what does Jesus mean?

Perhaps what Jesus means is simply living a godly life. In the earlier part of the book of Matthew, we are given the sermon on the mount. At the very beginning of the sermon on the mount, we are told about the attitudes. Each of these attitudes is attached to a reward.

The poor and spirit inherit the kingdom of heaven. Those who mourn will be comforted. The meek will inherit the earth. Those who hunger and thirst for righteousness will be satisfied. The merciful will receive mercy. The pure heart will see God. The peacemakers will be called sons of God. And those who are persecuted for righteousness sake will have the kingdom of heaven. Clearly, Jesus teaches and believes that our works will be rewarded. And so those treasures that we store up in heaven are stored by our purified hearts through the grace of God.

The final sentence of this passage is of great importance. It is sad where your treasure is there, your heart will be also. And so if we are attempting to lay up treasures for ourselves in heaven, then our hearts should Long for that home as well. And that is what it'll feel like to our home. These treasures will not feel like brand-new jewels that we somehow got. I believe they will feel more like an inheritance.

Do you have any family heirlooms? Perhaps you will be blessed with a family ring. Maybe you will inherit some family land. We have been given a very old Bible that contains the name of a deceased family member. The Bible has become very precious to us, like a treasure in our home. It sits displayed in our living room. This is speculation, admittedly, but I believe the treasures of heaven will feel more like an inheritance than a pirate's chest. Perhaps we can look at these different treasures and be reminded of how we achieve them. It may also be like looking back on old photos and remembering where we have been and what was accomplished by the grace of God.

On Earth As It Is In Heaven

It is important for us to consider how we can live in light of this truth. If heaven is our home, how does that change what we do here on earth? How does that change how we manage our own homes? I think that it changes everything for us. If we have the perspective that nothing here on earth is eternal value, then it changes how we look at those things.

We are tempted to spend far too much time worrying over temporary things. Granted, those worries are real and have a place. Your mortgage is an important thing to be concerned about. Whether or not you have a car to drive to work is of significant value. Having enough money in the bank in order to put food on the table matters.

But all of these things matter more than internal things, and we find ourselves in trouble. Losing nights of sleep and causing fights with our spouse is over financial worries and stripes do not enhance our lives here on earth. And they certainly do not store up treasures for us in heaven.

How would your life change if you spent more of your time thinking about heaven as your home than your earthly home? How much stress would be relieved if you focused more on the place that is prepared for you than managing and maintaining the place that you have prepared for yourself? Once again, I am not saying that these things on earth have no value. They do, and we ought to take care of them.

But there comes a significant change in our lives when we begin to think about heaven more often. If it is indeed truly our home, then it ought to capture our hearts. If that is where our treasure truly is, then the Bible says that is where our heart actually lies, so this poses an interesting question for us as believers. Where does your heart lie?

You can answer this question by looking at what does keep you up at night. Where do you spend most of your time? If there are arguments in your relationship, what are they surrounded by? It has been rightly said that you can look for your priorities in your checkbook. What are you spending all of your money on?

Changing our perspective to begin considering eternal things takes work. It is not a natural thing for us. In fact, it is a very supernatural thing to happen to us. We need the grace of God and the work of God to happen in our hearts. The whole process begins with prayer.

We need to begin to pray what Jesus prayed. We need to begin to think like he did. He was always thinking about the father and what was to come. Never to completely neglect what was happening right here in front of him on earth, but always with the end goal in mind. And so perhaps we need to begin praying for God to make us what is to come. Maybe we need some things to be removed from our lives so that we can focus more on heavenly things. Or maybe just the simple practice of praying Will daily. Remind us that this is not all there is to this world. There is a God who sits on his throat in heaven. And in his kingdom, there is a place prepared for us. There is a home waiting for us.

For Further Study

Read Matthew 6:19-33

Read John 14:1-11

Read 2 Corinthians 5:1-5

Read Psalm 23

Read Hebrews 13:7-16

DISCUSSION QUESTIONS

1. What kind of place do you think Jesus has prepared for us?

2. How does it make you feel that Jesus has done this for you?

3. What have we done to deserve this kind of mercy?

4. Do you think the place made for us is a mansion as is described in the King James Version of the Bible?

5. What kind of treasures will we lay up for ourselves in Heaven?

6. How do we lay up treasures for ourselves in Heaven?

7. What will we do with those treasures when we get them?

CHAPTER 7

THE HOPE OF THE BELIEVER

Hope is an interesting thing. It is something that everyone strives for. For some people, it is all too elusive. The lack of hope can change someone's outlook on life so much that they would be willing to end their own. The power of Hope cannot be understated. And so when the Bible teaches that heaven is our hope. It carries a lot of weight.

I read a story one time that powerfully illustrates what hope looks like. It was in an article by Gary Thomas in Christianity Today. It goes like this:

"As Vice President, George Bush represented the U.S. at the funeral of former Soviet leader Leonid Brezhnev. Bush was deeply moved by a silent protest carried out by Brezhnev's widow. She stood motionless by the coffin until seconds before it was closed. Then, just as the soldiers touched the lid, Brezhnev's wife performed an act of great courage and hope, a gesture that must surely rank as one of the most profound acts of civil disobedience ever committed: She reached down and made the sign of the cross on her husband's chest.

There, in the citadel of secular, atheistic power, the wife of the man who had run it all hoped that her husband was wrong. She hoped that there was another life and that that life was best represented by Jesus who died on the cross, and that the same Jesus might yet have mercy on her husband."

Hope changes everything. And it shines most brightly in the face of death. I have heard countless stories of men and women who, on their deathbed, look longingly to the sky and begin to smile as they take their last breaths. It is because their hope is becoming a reality. It is almost as if they can see their savior right then in that moment. So, let's take a moment to consider the hope that is found in heaven. What was taught by Christ is echoed by the Apostles.

But our citizenship is in heaven, and from it we await a Savior, the Lord Jesus Christ, who will transform our lowly body to be like his glorious body, by the power that enables him even to subject all things to himself.

Philippians 3:20, ESV

All of us are citizens of a country. This can be a difficult subject for some to discuss. This can be the very pride of others. Depending on the state of your country, you may have different feelings on the topic. But none of us can deny that we all belong to some country. When the national anthem is played, it moves us. When we see the colors of our flags, we are stirred to a response.

You can probably see this most clearly in the Olympic games. In this event that happens every couple of years all nations from across the globe come together to cheer for their country. What is interesting is that as men and women around the world watch the Olympic games on TV, they probably don't actually know the contestants. They may not have any idea who they are or where they come from in their country. But the fact that they bear the country's colors means that they will cheer for them. They will scream to the top of their lungs and support not only the person but also the country that they represent.

There is an immense amount of pride that comes with knowing and being Honored by the country that you come from and represent. No matter what country you have to call home here on earth, the Bible teaches that heaven is our ultimate country. It is the place in which our citizenship truly rests. And just as a good citizen here on earth honors and serves their country, so we ought to honor and serve our country in heaven. This new citizenship that we gain by faith in Jesus affects everything. And we can be confident of this citizenship because of Christ.

Have you ever lost confidence in yourself or someone else?Maybe over a little thing like missing a step or struggling to find a straw. Maybe over a big thing like being lied to or even cheated on. It's painful when we place our confidence in something, and it fails us.

In the passage above, Paul shows us why our confidence should be in Christ alone. Our confidence in Christ should lead us to press on and press in.

Typically, in Paul's writing, that would have been the end of the letter. However, we have a strange grammatical situation happening here. Paul begins a brand new thought with the word finally. But this isn't the only finally in the letter. The oldest preacher trick in the book! It's almost as if Paul was about to finish this letter when compelled by the Spirit to continue on.

Whatever the situation, here we have more of God's precious Word to us, His people. We can have confidence in Christ according to Philippians 2:1-10. Again, we find Paul giving the command to rejoice. It's no wonder why this letter is called the letter of joy. Time and time again, Paul gives reason to rejoice. With chains on his hands, division in the church, false teachers creeping in, and Epaphroditus nearing death, Paul still points us to rejoice.

This passage is no different. Here's the issue at hand: There is a group called Judaizers who are Jewish people who teach that in order to be saved, you must believe in Jesus and keep the Jewish law, in particular the law regarding circumcision. Paul, being a Jewish person who is following Jesus, confronts this group in a handful of his letters. He does so very strongly in this one.

He says to beware of the dogs. When we hear this, we may think Paul is just being mean.

But when the gentiles hear this, they hear something different. Jewish people would often refer to Gentiles as dogs. Almost as if they were lesser people because of their heritage. Paul is now using that term pointedly towards these Judiazers instead. It's not your heritage that saves you, but your faith in Jesus alone.

He also calls them evil workers. This is not Paul saying that they do evil things but that their motives are evil. Once again, Paul is turning the tables on the Judaizers because this is a term that they would normally use to describe the Gentiles.

Finally, he uses the phrase concision. This one is the most pointed claim of all because it means those who mutilate their flesh. The sign of the covenant (not the covenant itself) was circumcision. If you were one of God's people in the OT, then you had to be circumcised.

Paul is taking the very thing that they hold most dear and calling it mutilation of their flesh.

Maybe you're thinking, Paul needs to chill out! How can he justify speaking so harshly?

Look back at Philippians 1:15-16. Paul had little to say about those who were preaching the Gospel with wrongful motives.

But here's the difference: these Judaizers were not preaching the Gospel. The message they brought was insidious and deceiving, leading others to place their faith in their works.

To be clear, Paul was not trying to be mean, but he was surely aware that his words would sting. And for good reason. It's for their own sake and the sake of the Philippian church that Paul wanted to make clear what the Gospel is.

In verse 3, it says... "For we are circumcised..." This is a dramatic statement signifying the great reversal that has happened among the Jews and Gentiles. No longer is the sign of the covenant a circumcision of your flesh but of your heart. Paul makes a special plea to the Jewish congregation being convinced of that false teaching in Philippians 4-6. He basically says that there's no one more Jewish than Paul!

Like if George Washington were eating Apple Pie watching a baseball game, it doesn't get more American than that! If anyone were to have confidence in their flesh, if anyone was going to change the gospel to include circumcision, it would have been Paul.

Notice how Paul views his status, both what he was born with and the keeping of the law in Philippians 2:7-8. Paul had an Isaiah 64:6 view of his own righteousness, as impressive as it was: "All our righteousnesses are as filthy rags." His confidence was not in his flesh. It was in Christ, according to verse 9. There, he makes it plain that our righteousness is of God by faith. Like what it says in 2 Corinthians 5:21, " For he hath made him be sin for us, who knew no sin; that we might be made the righteousness of God in him." Or elsewhere in Romans 5:6-9 it says, "For when we were yet without strength, in due time Christ died for the ungodly. For scarcely for a righteous man will one die: yet peradventure for a good man some would even dare to die. But God commendeth his love toward us, in that, while we were yet sinners, Christ died for us. Much more than, being now justified by his blood, we shall be saved from wrath through him. . . For as by one man's disobedience many were made sinners, so by the obedience of one shall many be made righteous."

Friend, when Jesus died on the cross, He paid the full penalty for sin. For as many as would believe in Him, He has justified them by his blood. A few hundred years ago, when people began to travel west to start settlements, one of the great dangers they faced was. I heard a story about a man who was traveling west. Lo and behold, while he was on his way, a wildfire began to burn. There was no river to cross and no safe place to be found. So the man lit a match and burnt the ground in front of him. As the ground burned before him and the flames from far off crept closer, he circled his wagon on top of where the burned grass was left. Fire will not reburn its own ashes. Eventually, the man found himself surrounded by flames, and yet he was safe. The ground he and his family were planted on had already been scorched. We stand on the scorched ground of Christ's work for us!

Friend, if you are reading this and you have not placed your faith in Jesus, please know that this offer is available to you. His nail-scarred hands are open and ready to save you if you will place your full trust in Him. This is our confidence! And this is why Paul is adamant that we reject any kind of Gospel that adds to the work of Christ for our salvation.

It's a confidence that we will know Him and his excellencies (v. 8, 10). It's a confidence in the resurrection power that is in us by His grace (v. 10). It's a confidence that sustains us when we enter into the fellowship of His sufferings (v. 10). It's a confidence that transforms us into his image, even unto death (v. 10). It's a confidence that hopes in the resurrection to come for all of those who are in Christ (v. 11). Right now, I have to ask you, where is your confidence?

What are you doing or trusting in order to earn God's love? Your Christian heritage. Your consistency in Bible reading or prayer. Your clean record. Your service to the church

Your biblical knowledge. All of these things are good, but they are no defense before an Almighty God.

When you stand before God, and He asks you to defend yourself, what would you say? What's the first and second thing that comes to mind? Friend, if it's not Jesus and only Jesus, give up that false Gospel and cling to Jesus alone! Our confidence is in Christ! And this ought to lead us to press on and press in according to Philippians 2:12-14.

If this is all true, and if all of our works bear no weight on whether or not we are saved, what's the point? Why would we follow the example to "press on towards the mark"? Don't miss the significance of verse 12, which says, "I am apprehended by Christ." In other words, Jesus has taken hold of me. Brothers and sisters, our confidence in Christ compels us to act for His sake. He has taken hold of us!

This is not perfect obedience (Philippians 2:13). "I'm not perfect. I haven't arrived. But here's one thing I've learned." Leaving the guilt of the past and clinging to the hope of the future.

Can you imagine the difficulty of this for Paul? Remember his pedigree? "Concerning zeal, persecuting the church." Surely, Paul dealt with immense grief and guilt when thinking about his life before Jesus. And yet, he made it a point to leave it behind. Each and every day, he puts to death the guilt of his past by the power of the Gospel and presses on.

Let me say it this way: Jesus has paid your debt for each and every sin. You've been forgiven. So, what is it that you cannot forgive yourself for? What guilt or shame does the devil throw in your face? Forget those things that are behind! Are there lessons to be learned and lasting consequences for our mistakes? Absolutely, but guilt and shame have no place in the life of the believer.

Not only did he leave the guilt of the past, but he replaced that guilt with glory and pressed on toward the goal (Philippians 2:14). What is the prize? What is that high calling? It's what can only be found in glory. Perfect obedience to a glorious God, unhindered by sin.

Paul put all he had into ''working out his salvation with fear and trembling," trusting that it was "God which worketh in him to will and to do His good pleasure."

Paul's language here is that of a runner refusing to look behind him and keeping his eyes on the goal. So let me ask, what are you looking back at? Maybe for you, it's not your sinful past but past successes? We have a temptation to become satisfied or complacent in our growth.

"I've read the whole Bible." "I've done all the studies." "I've led people to Jesus." "I've served my time in the nursery or youth ministry." Friend, do not let up. We must not slow down.

Christ has said, "The harvest is plentiful, but the laborers are few." Let us be counted among the few.

If you're exhausted by the work or overwhelmed by the race before you, take heart. You're not meant to do this alone. You can press into your community of faith according to Philippians 3:15-4:1. Notice the change in language here: up to this point, he has been explaining his experience and his desire to press on. Now, he invites the Philippian church to join him.

He calls all those who will join him in his pursuit of spiritual maturity (v. 15). He calls for unity as he has done so before (v. 16). He calls for them to follow him and any others who serve as an example (v. 17). Part of the application here for us is to be men and women worthy of following, but I want to draw out a bigger picture idea here.

Paul is calling these believers to live their lives with one another. Watching each other, following each other, having the same mind, showing each other where they have not yet reached maturity. Christian, you cannot do this life alone. There's no room for lone rangers and no job description for special agents in God's kingdom.

Friend, practice gathering quickly and scattering slowly. When you go to church, there is a brother who is at his wit's end. Across the pew, there is a sister who feels alone. Down the aisle, there is someone who desperately needs to know Jesus but feels unwelcome in His church. I'm not asking you to stay for hours or to let whatever is in your crockpot burn. But I am encouraging you to be the one who reaches out and creates a sanctifying community.

Here's the reality. We're always being disciplined by someone. If we don't step up and discipline one another, then someone else will fill in the gap. Remember those whom Paul warned us about at the beginning; he brings them up again here (Philippians 2:18-19).

When you hear "enemies of the cross," you may think of devil-worshiping atheists, but this is not who Paul is referring to. It's the Judiazers. Those who look like Christians, talk like Christians, act like Christians, and mostly believe like Christians, and yet they have attacked the beauty of the cross by trying to take away its power.

It's not the agnostic or Buddhist that Paul is warning against. It's the wolf in sheep's clothing. So church, your brothers and sisters need you.

They need you to be that example. They need you to initiate a relationship with them that will do them spiritual good. They need you to spend time walking through difficult things with them. They need you to learn how to fail and to succeed.

Not many of us are in danger of apostasy, but we are constantly in danger of the slow drift away. The illustration that Paul gives for the community we are supposed to be a part of is one he has used already (Philippians 2:20-21; 1:27). Remember, the Greek word that's translated has the imagery of citizenship. Instead of using this just to illustrate, he is using it as our hope and encouragement to press on and press in. There is coming a day when the pressing on will end, and our bodies will be glorified. (v. 21)

But until that day, Paul has one final thought for us. Philippians 4:1 says to stand fast.

With the strongest display of love, to remind them he is not bringing condemnation and judgment, but pastoral care: he says to stand fast in the Lord. We've got our marching orders this morning at church. Place your full confidence in Christ. Press on towards the goal of spiritual maturity. Press into a community of believers. Stand fast in those pursuits.

In what area is God leading you to respond to this today? Do you have something you've been placing your confidence in other than Jesus? Have you grown stagnant in your spiritual walk? Maybe you need to commit yourself to a local church and are interested in uniting one today. Reach out to one or go to a worship service soon.

Blessed be the God and Father of our Lord Jesus Christ! According to his great mercy, he has caused us to be born again to a living hope through the resurrection of Jesus Christ from the dead, to an inheritance that is imperishable, undefiled, and unfading, kept in heaven for you, who by God's power are being guarded through faith for a salvation ready to be revealed in the last time.

1 Peter 1:4-5, ESV

I've started working out, and there comes a point in every workout where I decide will I finish this one or not. In a pathetic defeat this past Monday, while my video instructor was encouraging me to do more pushups, I was lying out of breath on the floor, and I called it quits.

What helps me when those moments come is when I can look up and see the end. If that little red bar is almost at the end, I can already feel the relief, and I can power through. In the text above, Peter is going to encourage us to lift up our heads and see the end. We can praise God through hardship because of our great salvation.

This letter is circulating through the churches in what is modern-day Turkey. It is received as pastoral care from a trusted man of God and leader in the Church, Peter. The first thing he wants to remind them of is the Gospel. Church, this has got to be the foundation of any and all counsel that we give to our friends and our family. If we truly want to care for them, we've got to point them to Jesus first.

If someone is struggling financially, remind them that the owner of all creation has set his love on them and bought them at such a high price. He can surely handle their financial situation.

After you've rooted that advice in the gospel, then transition on to the how-to's of building a budget. If you don't soothe the soul with the Gospel, you'll train it to self-soothe by the law. What a dangerous place that is to be.

In verse 3, Peter calls their salvation a "lively hope." This just doesn't do the Greek word justice, as if our hope is just spunky or peppy. A better translation is "living hope." That's exactly what it is! Our hope is in someone who has done the impossible. He was once dead and is now alive. Take a glimpse at other religions to find out who their hope is in. If it's in a person, that person is dead or dying.

That's not the case with Jesus. He has conquered the one enemy that no one can escape. Death itself. Our hope is a living hope. Without the resurrection, our faith would be in vain (1 Corinthians 15:14). Let's trace this thought out. Why would Jesus have to resurrect? Wouldn't our sins be paid for by His death alone? Isn't that what saves us?

We sing this, right? "What can wash away my sins, nothing but the blood of Jesus!"

It's made crystal clear in Hebrews 9:22: "Without shedding of blood, there is no remission."

If that's all it took, then why the resurrection? Would our faith really be completely in vain if Jesus was never raised from the dead? Jesus had to be raised from the dead for at least three reasons.

First, He said he would (Matthew 16:21; Mark 8:31). "And he began to teach them that the Son of Man must suffer many things and be rejected by the elders and the chief priests and the scribes and be killed, and after three days rise again." It's proof that His death accomplished what He said it would. Think about it. Anyone could make the claim that when I die, your sins will be forgiven. But on what basis would we believe them? Like with the gospel of Mark, why would we believe that Jesus is the son of God? His miraculous life is the evidence.

The resurrection is wonderful proof for us of what Jesus accomplished for us on the cross. Let's finish the argument from 1 Corinthians 15:20-22. In the death of Christ, we have the death of sin and the ability to put to death our own sinful flesh. Praise God! But the story here is incomplete. As we share His death, we also must share

His resurrected life. As much as we need the death of sin, we need the newness of life!

Without the resurrection, we'd be like a man found at sea by the coastal guard. What if all they did was toss down a life preserver and then leave him? Sure, they kept him alive, but they didn't give him life! We have the beautiful privilege of having a living hope to hold onto. One that gives us life.

Like when there's a prize in your cereal box, Peter says, there's more! If the death of death wasn't enough. If new life in Christ wasn't enough. There's this incredible inheritance that waits for you. Don't miss the word inheritance. It's given to you because you've been adopted into the family. It's not something you've earned. It's grace upon the grace of your salvation.

There are rewards and crowns that are spoken about for the believer elsewhere. That's not what Peter is talking about here.

It is "incorruptible." a better translation may be imperishable, considering the following word essentially means incorruptible. There's reasonable debate here. Peter would use that idea right after discussing the resurrection of Christ. This inheritance cannot die.

It is undefiled. Unlike baseball pants that are never as white as when you first buy them, the inheritance that awaits us doesn't have a single spot or blemish. It is perfect.

It does not fade away. This is a wonderful thing to ponder because we have eternity to spend with this inheritance. If it faded away, even at an astonishingly slow rate, it would eventually be gone. This is not true with our inheritance in Christ. It will last longer than the stack of napkins in your dash or the box of sauces from fast food places in your cabinets.

It is reserved in heaven for you. This means that the inheritance we're waiting for is not heaven itself. Although heaven fits this description. It's something in heaven. So what is it?

Is it the room that Christ made for us? Is it the unfading crown of glory 1 Peter 5:4. Is it the community of believers that are there? Is it everything that we've mentioned so far? All the individual things that make up heaven?

We could wonder and dream all night about this coming day, but we know this. It is not less than God Himself. While all the other things of heaven will be there for our enjoyment, no doubt. The greatest part of heaven, the greatest hope we have, the greatest thing we have to look forward to is God Himself.

It is by him that we are kept by the power of God 1 Peter 2:4. Is there greater security known to man? I read that and think of the imagery that Jesus gives; that no man can pluck us from His hand. Salvation ready to be revealed. We see this concept all throughout the Christian life. Theologians call it "already but not yet." We are already declared righteous before the Father, but we're not experiencing that moment yet. We are already set free from sin, but we haven't experienced full deliverance. We are already saved; our name is in the Lambs' Book of Life, but we haven't yet seen that salvation come to fulfillment. In essence, Peter is saying look up and keep your head up. No matter the trial or the difficulty. In good times and bad, we have a great salvation and inheritance ahead.

Heaven is our Hope

We always thank God, the Father of our Lord Jesus Christ, when we pray for you, since we heard of your faith in Christ Jesus and of the love that you have for all the saints, because of the hope laid up for you in heaven.

Colossians 1:3-5, ESV

It is the place where we will rest from the troubles of this life. It is the place where we will be rewarded for our efforts. It is the place where we will commune with God, like Adam and Eve in the Garden. It is the place where we will see our Savior's nail-scarred hands and hear from Him. It is the place where there will be no more death, tears, or sorrow. There is a great Hymn entitled On Jordan's Stormy Banks I Stand that captures this reality in a beautiful way. It goes like this:

On Jordan's stormy banks, I stand, and cast a wistful eye to Canaan's fair and happy land, where my possessions lie. No chilling winds or poisonous breath can reach that healthful shore; sickness and sorrow, pain and death, are felt and feared no more. When I shall reach that happy place, I'll be forever blessed, for I shall see my Father's face, and in his bosom rest. I am bound for the promised land, I am bound for the promised land; oh, who will come and go with me? I am bound for the promised land.

The hope of Heaven is one of the greatest comforts of the believer. This is accompanied by the hope that we have in the One whom Heaven holds. It's like when I realized that I needed glasses. Part of that experience is seeing your current vision in comparison to your vision with glasses on. When they did that, I laughed. It was pure joy. That moment made me long for heaven.

I remember sitting, waiting on the doctor to do one final thing. While I waited, I stared at a blurry sign with a smile on my face, thinking of the day when that would no longer be blurry.

John, 1 John 2:28-3:3, rushes us towards that day as we think about when Jesus will return and make all things new. I bet you can't get what John will encourage us to do until that day. Abide in Christ until He comes.

Remembering earlier in John, he talks about the antichrists in light of the Antichrist.

John warned us about their deceit and the pain of finding out who they were. He had already started thinking about the end times when he mentioned that this was the "last hour" or "last time." And now he is pointing his finger right at it and offering us a piece of encouragement in light of the danger of the antichrists.

He says first that Christ will come in Righteousness (1 John 2:28-29). When I read these verses, they make me a little uncomfortable. Verse 28 says that we are to have confidence and not be ashamed before His coming. But when I think about His coming, there is a moment of fear. Let's think about it together by reflecting on Revelation 19:11-16.

Veres 11 says that when Jesus comes, He comes to judge and make war based on his righteous standard. Veres 12 says that His purity and royalty are unmatched. Verse 13 teaches that His clothes are dipped in blood and is the very word of God. Verse 14 goes on to say that He is the commander of all of the armies of heaven. Then, in verse 15, he is shown as the leader of this holy army. And He comes bearing a sword that will strike down all nations; with an iron rod, he will rule them. And "he will tread the winepress of the fierceness and wrath of Almighty God."

Imagine Him coming; surely, at least, a twinge of fear is in your heart. Why? - Because verse 29 doesn't seem to describe us. Who among us is righteous? Even today, if you were to tally up your sins, they would wreck you before the Father. If Jesus' coming is the beginning of an all-out war against unrighteousness, then friends, we're in trouble! We're on the wrong side of the war.

This should strike a holy fear in us until we remember what Paul says in Romans 4:5

"But to him that worketh not, but believeth on him that justifieth the ungodly, his faith is counted for righteousness." Get this, friend. The righteousness of Jesus strikes fear into our hearts as we consider our own unrighteousness. This righteousness is what is credited to accounts. This is mind-boggling. This is wonderful. This is the Gospel!

Our bank account reads debtor. We're in the red. And yet, when we place our faith in Jesus, His righteousness is credited to our account. The debt is canceled. It's no wonder, then, that we are told to abide in Him. Where else can we go? Can our own goodness suffice? Can our family's legacy save us? Can our church attendance, non-profit giving, or hours spent on the mission field produce enough righteousness to cancel our debt?

No! The only safe place for the Christian is Christ. And praise God, His arms are open wide. When He comes in righteousness, may we be found in Him. John continues on to say that Christ will come in Love (1 John 3:1-3). I love the two-sided nature of the gospel message.

There is the legal. Debt that is canceled. A broken law that has been punished. It's black and white. Almost clinical. And my mind loves it.

But there's more to the gospel than just the legality of it all. There is the relational side as well. You who were once far away are now near. You were strangers; now you're citizens. As this passage says, you were orphans, and now your sons and daughters. The legal side satisfies my mind, but the relational side satisfies my soul.

This wonderful new standing (now righteous) and a new relationship (sons and daughters) prepares us for this ultimate goal (v. 2) that "we shall be like Him." The righteousness that is credited to our account will be made real in our lives. Our daily war with sin will be over. I can barely hold back tears when I sing this song! "Dear dying Lamb, Thy precious blood Shall never lose its power, Till all the ransomed ones of God Be saved, to sin no more:" We shall be like Him, not just in the legal sense, but also in the relational sense.

Consider the perfect relationship that exists within God. The Father, Son, and Spirit perfectly love one another. And if we will be like Him, our relationship with God will be perfect. Without hindrance. Think of all of the things that make relationships hard right now: Miscommunication, hurts, grudges, assumptions, etc. None of those will exist between us and God.

Think of your frustrations with God now (and don't act like they aren't there). There are times when you feel like you could use a little more communication. There are times when you want a sense of closeness and intimacy. Right now, our relationship with God is not in the perfect state it will be because we're still sinners struggling with our sinful flesh. But one day, when he returns, "we will be like Him."

Brothers and sisters, this ought to stir up in you an intense hope for the future (v. 3). We've made it full circle now: This legal and relational truth of the Gospel produces in us a striving for purity. Go back with me to verses 28-29 that produced fear and read them in light of the gospel.

Where does our confidence come from? How can we stand unashamed? Where is the righteousness' root? And in verse 3, what has made us pure? The hope of the gospel that comes through abiding in Him.

On Earth As It Is In Heaven

The hope of Heaven changes everything about how we live our lives on earth. It changes how much trust we put in earthly things. Our finances, family, and jobs are the leading causes of stress in our lives. But what if we viewed all of those things through the lens of Heaven?

If we become Heavenly minded, we won't be as worried about how much our next paycheck will be. We know that if God has prepared a place for us there, He will surely take care of us while we are here. With the hope of Heaven, even the most devastating loss of a family member cannot destroy us. If they are in Christ, then we will have the joy of seeing them again. Our jobs, whether they are fulfilling or not on earth, matter less. For we have a greater job, a heavenly job, to attend to.

Be intentional about putting your whole life in the frame of Heaven. Let that future hope shape how you live today. Let it inspire hope in every aspect of your life. This incredible promise is not so far removed that you cannot enjoy it right now. Pray with your Savior that even the hope that exists in Heaven will be on earth right now.

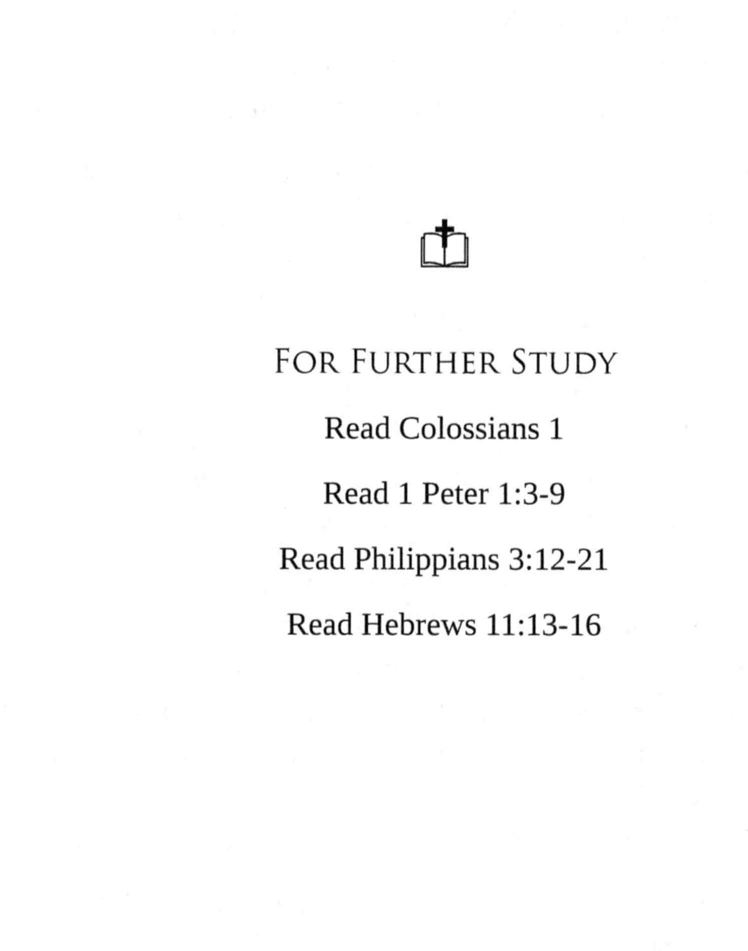

For Further Study

Read Colossians 1

Read 1 Peter 1:3-9

Read Philippians 3:12-21

Read Hebrews 11:13-16

DISCUSSION QUESTIONS

1. Why is Heaven the hope of the believer?

2. How often do you think about Heaven?

3. How would your life change if you thought of it more often?

4. What does it mean that Heaven is where our citizenship lies?

5. In what ways does our heavenly citizenship change our earthly citizenship?

6. What does it mean that Heaven is our inheritance?

7. How does our heavenly inheritance change how we view our earthly inheritance?

Chapter 8

The Present Heaven

Theologically, there is so much to learn about our heavenly home. As we looked through the Old Testament, Jesus' teachings, and the rest of the New Testament, we have learned incredible truths to behold. But now the time has come to begin asking and answering the questions about what Heaven will be like. What will be there? Who will be there? What will we do when we get there?

These chapters will not provide the answer to every question you have, but we can get a sense of what Heaven will be like as we study the Word of God in Revelations 4 and 5. What we will discover in these two incredible chapters is that the present Heaven is a place of perfect worship of God. Through the written experience of John, we will see with the eyes of our hearts the throne room of God and the worship that takes place around it.

If you were paying attention, you'll notice that I said, "the present Heaven" and not just, "Heaven." The reason is that the Bible presents two "heavens," if you will. There is Heaven as it is now and a future heaven to come. Most of us have been taught that heaven will be a place with pearly white gates and streets of gold. But did you know that that is actually a description of the new heaven, or more precisely, the New Jerusalem, to come? (Rev. 21:1-2, 18-21)

Let me put this on a timeline for you that is essentially presented in Revelation as a whole. There is the Present Heaven (which we will study in Revelation 4-5) and the present Earth and Jerusalem that will endure judgment (Revelation 6-18). After this, Jesus will leave the present heaven and reign on the present earth in present Jerusalem (Revelation 19). Then, there is a great and final judgment (Revelation 20). In the midst of the great and final judgment, the present earth and present are destroyed with fire (2 Peter 3:10-12)

The new heaven and the new earth with its new Jerusalem don't enter until after all of this in ch. 21-22. In upcoming chapters, we will dive into those details, but for now, we're going to focus on what we know of the Present Heaven. We read in Psalm 11:4, "The Lord is in his holy temple; the Lord's throne is in heaven." The Apostle John was blessed to enter, by vision, into the throne room of the Lord. Let's go there together by His Word.

THE THRONE ROOM

If you look back in Chapter 1, you'll discover that this whole journey for John began in chains on the Isle of Patmos. One Sunday morning, He was in the Spirit, and someone spoke to him. That someone is later found to be Jesus, "the one who died and alive forevermore." Jesus told John, "Write what you see - the things which are and the things that are to come" (Revelation 1:19). This verse, along with verse 1, says this book is a revelation of Jesus. This is the interpretative tool of Revelation. The whole book reveals Jesus as He interacts with what is right now and what He will do in the days to come.

There is a great debate on when that shift takes place, a conversation for another day. For now, let's simply understand Chapter 4 in light of the interpretive tool. The throne room tells us about how Jesus interacts with us now in the present heaven. Take a look around the room with me, and let's take in the sights.

At once I was in the Spirit, and behold, a throne stood in heaven, with one seated on the throne. And he who sat there had the appearance of jasper and carnelian, and around the throne was a rainbow that had the appearance of an emerald.

Revelation 4:2-3, ESV

He sees a great throne and someone sitting on it. The one sitting on the throne is not given human features, but His brilliance is described. Jasper is a transparent stone, like a diamond. If a light is shown through it, it will display a whole host of colors. Carnelian is a red stone. This is a powerful color. Perhaps it is suggesting the justice of the one who is seated on the throne.

Around the throne was a rainbow. Take time to note the significance of this in light of the coming destruction of the world by fire. The God who brought the covenant to Noah to never destroy the earth by a flood (Genesis 9:8-17) is poised and ready to create a new earth by fire. An interesting note about the rainbow is given. It is said that it looked like an emerald, which is a green stone. Maybe, as it showed around him, it brought to mind the Garden of Eden. Regardless of the exact meaning of the imagery, the brilliance is undeniable.

The throne and the One who sat on it were surrounded by others according to verse 4. 24 Thrones surround the one great one. No description is given of these lesser thrones because none is needed. They are not the focus. These 24 thrones have 24 elders occupying those seats. They are given human features with a white garment (signifying purity) and crowns of gold upon the heads. Who are these elders? We cannot know for sure, but it would make sense to consider the 12 sons of Israel and the 12 apostles who make up the 24 elders. Since they don't give attention to themselves, we won't spend too much time speculating either.

One final description of the throne is given in the following verses.

Thunder and lightning reveal the great power of the One who occupies the central throne. The seven torches of fire are said to be the seven spirits of God. Once again, a variety of interpretations can be offered, but let me offer this simple one. Traditionally, the number 7 in the Bible is considered the number of perfection or completion. The seven 'spirits of God' could very well represent the perfect Holy Spirit surrounding the throne of the Father.

Finally, before the throne is a sea of glass or the crystal sea. Not a sea made of water, but a great translucent floor is present before the throne. The throne room is designed to allow the brilliance of light to flood it at all times. We could spend hours just trying to soak in the Throne Room, and one day, we will, but let's move on to the action of the room. What is happening here?

If there was any doubt in your mind, the One seated on the throne is called "the Lord God Almighty" and "the One who lives forever and ever." The 24 elders do not occupy their thrones as God does. They leave theirs and bow before the One true King. They even cast their crowns at his feet and give Him glory.

Notice, too, the creatures that surround the throne. More than any other section in Chapter 4, there is great debate over the representation of these creatures. It's possible they are just creatures, but unlikely, given the clear imagery throughout the book of Revelation. Matthew Henry and others believe they are representations of Christians. "By their many eyes [they show] vigilance . . . By their lion-like courage, their great labor and diligence (in which they resemble the ox), their prudence and discretion becoming men, and their sublime affections and speculations, by which they mount up with wings like eagles towards heaven." Others say that they are angels from Ezekiel 1:4-10. Like the elders, the creatures are not the central focus, but God is. Even they, whomever they represent, give God all glory and honor.

This Throne Room is not all the present Heaven consists of, but it is the focal point. The Present Heaven is a place of perfect worship. And when we stand before the throne, unhindered by visions and unhindered by sin, we will worship God perfectly in spirit and in truth.

THE LAMB WHO WAS SLAIN

Heaven is a place of perfect worship. The four creatures and the 24 elders fell down before God the Father and the Holy Spirit and worshiped

Him there. Chapter 4 highlights those two persons of the Trinity. As we make our way into Chapter 5, the Son will be introduced as the Lamb of God.

Then I saw in the right hand of him who was seated on the throne a scroll written within and on the back, sealed with seven seals. And I saw a mighty angel proclaiming with a loud voice, "Who is worthy to open the scroll and break its seals?" And no one in heaven or on earth or under the earth was able to open the scroll or to look into it, and I began to weep loudly because no one was found worthy to open the scroll or to look into it.

Revelation 5:1-4, ESV

The drama that unfolds in Heaven during the vision of John centers around the scroll in the hand of God. Remembering the One sitting on the throne is God the Father, the scroll is simply what it sounds like, a message. In biblical times, if a king were to send a message or make a decree, that message was written down, rolled into a scroll, and sealed with wax. The king would drop wax and press his signet ring into it as it dried. This would signify to the reader that it was a direct message from the king.

Did you notice how many times this message from the King was sealed? Like with the seven spirits of God, the seven seals tell us that the intent is to show perfection or completion. So, the message of God is perfectly sealed. All of heaven wanted to read what was on the scroll! The new message of God to His people. What will He say? What is to come?

One of the angels asks the question in the heart of every citizen of the kingdom of God, "Who can open it?" The only one who has the authority to open the scrolls is the one to whom it is addressed. John looked around, and there was no one to be found. No one stands up and says he is worthy. John's response is telling of his deep love for God and His Word. He records himself as having fallen down and weeping.

I was challenged by this verse because John embodies Psalm 119:18-20 which says, "Open my eyes, that I may behold wondrous things out of your law. I am a sojourner on the earth; hide not your commandments from me! My soul is consumed with longing for your rules at all times." Don't miss this response of the one in the presence of God. He cannot stand the anticipation. He is distraught at the thought of not being able to hear the message. He is desperate for the Word of God. I'm challenged by this because the Word of God that I have access to isn't sealed. I'm not waiting for someone worthy to open it. The Father has addressed it to me. I can hear from Him any time I want to, and I neglect that privilege.

And yet, I like John, standing in His presence every day. Not in the same way, don't get me wrong. But if I were more actively aware of the presence of God in my life and the gift of His word to me, it would change my whole outlook on reading the Bible. I challenge you to grow that awareness in your own life. Start your days with a simple prayer of, "God, I praise you that you are with me today. Give me a hunger for your word." John's weeping doesn't last long as he is comforted by one of the 24 elders.

Imagine one of the men sitting on the thrones surrounding the great throne of God, offering his comfort to you. What a moment of grace John experienced as his eyes were fixed on his one and only hope: the lamb which looked as if he had been slain. Two names are given to the one who is worthy. The first is the Lion of the Tribe of Judah. It originates in Genesis 49:9-10 which says, "Judah is a lion's cub; from the prey, my son, you have gone up. He stooped down; he crouched as a lion and as a lioness; who dares rouse him? The scepter shall not depart from Judah, nor the ruler's staff from between his feet, until tribute comes to him; and to him shall be the obedience of the peoples." The prophecy here states that a great ruler from the Lion Tribe of Judah will arise.

The second title given to the Worthy One is the Root of David. This name originates in Isaiah 11:1, which says, "There shall come forth a shoot from the stump of Jesse, and a branch from his roots shall bear fruit." Jesus accepts this title in Revelation 22:16, where he says, "I, Jesus, have sent my angel to testify to you about these things for the churches. I am the root and the descendant of David, the bright morning star." There is no doubt the One who is worthy to open the scroll is Jesus.

The message is addressed to Him! This doesn't mean that it is for Him to read and Him alone. Like Ezekiel was given a scroll in Ezekiel 3, it was for Him to see and then proclaim. This scroll is for Jesus' eyes first but not His eyes only. It is a message to be shared with all of God's people. And now He enters the scene in an unexpected way. When our minds think of the Son of God, they may more naturally picture the Lion, but here He is depicted as a Lamb.

And between the throne and the four living creatures and among the elders I saw a Lamb standing, as though it had been slain, with seven horns and with seven eyes, which are the seven spirits of God sent out into all the earth. And he went and took the scroll from the right hand of him who was seated on the throne.

Revelation 5:6-7, ESV

The worthy One is given one last title: a Lamb that looks as if it had been slain. This is of massive importance because the imagery of a sacrificial lamb flows all the way through the Bible. Levitcus 4 describes that the offering for sin was to be a spotless lamb. Isaiah 53 says that it is by His wounds that we are healed. Hebrews 9:22 says that without the shedding of blood, there is no forgiveness of sins. John the Baptist says of Jesus, "Behold, the Lamb of God who takes away the sin of the world. This Worthy One, this mighty Lion of Judah, this descendent of the great King David, displays His power in humility. He comes as a slain lamb.

How does this make Him worthy to open the scroll and declare the Word?He is the very Word of God, and He has fulfilled every will of God. There is no one more worthy of this task than Jesus. The description of the lamb raises some questions with his seven horns and seven eyes, and it says that these are representative of the seven spirits of God. Last week, we talked about how this would be symbolic of the complete or perfect spirit of God and how He rested on Jesus, but let's see it from another place in Scripture for some confirmation. Going back to Isaiah 11:1-2 we read, " There shall come forth a shoot from the stump of Jesse, and a branch from his roots shall bear fruit And the Spirit of the Lord shall rest upon him, the Spirit of wisdom and understanding, the Spirit of counsel and might, the Spirit of knowledge and the fear of the Lord." Jesus, the Lion of Judah, the Root of David, the Lamb of God, He alone is worthy to open the scroll and He takes action to receive it

If you're like me, you're dying to know what's on the scroll! What is contained within its pages? What is the message of God the Father proclaimed by the crucified Son by the power of the Holy Spirit? Sadly, this scroll is not directly mentioned again in the Book of Revelation except for its seals. The seven seals are clearly described in chapters 6-8. Each one of them contains the judgment of God as they are broken. So before the scroll is read, Jesus breaks the seal of the judgment of God on mankind. After this point, the scroll is not mentioned again. There is a different scroll called the "little scroll" in chapter 10.

So, this scroll is one of two things. It is essentially the rest of Revelation that describes the end of time and the new that is to come, which Jesus must enact. Or it is later referred to as a book instead of a scroll because it is unscrolled. The book that is mentioned many times towards the end of Revelation is the Lamb's Book of Life. (Revelation 20:11-15) Regardless of where you land on that debate, the main point here is that Jesus, the central focus of the action of Heaven and the Word of God, is driving it all. Seeing the Worthy One in His proper place, ready to open the scroll, all of heaven breaks out in worship!

The elders and creatures fall down and worship, not the One on the throne alone, but the Lamb as well. Jesus, the Son of God, who did not regard equality with God as a thing to be grasped (Philippians 2:6), now receives the full worship He is owed. Jesus, like the Father, is God. And as the rest of the book of Revelation will reveal, all people will one day bow before Him (Philippians 2:10-11).

The bowls of incense draw our minds back to the Old Testament, where incense was continually burning in the Tabernacle. Now, it is described as the prayers of the saints being lifted up in worship. Then they sang a new song. Don't miss this. They have been with God in Heaven for years and centuries, and they are still singing new songs for new reasons. We can have a static view of heaven that has us singing "Holy, Holy, Holy" on repeat. But no, we will be learning reason after reason to worship God! And here's the reason for Heaven's worship on that day.

If it is said of the Father, Holy, Holy, Holy, to the Son, we sing, Worthy, Worthy, Worthy! By the end of this worship service, all of creation is joining in. So as to fulfill the saying of Jesus that even the rocks will cry out if we remain silent (Luke 19:40).

On Earth As It Is In Heaven

Let's draw from this heavenly scene a few lessons about what the present heaven is like. God is still speaking, and we will hang on to his every word. I mentioned it before, but it bears repeating; the desperation of God's people for God's word is an example to follow and a hope to look forward to. We will commune with the Father in perfect harmony, and He will speak to us with clarity that we have never experienced before.

Jesus is still central to our worship. Like our worship here, Jesus will be the centerpiece of it all. This will not be to the detriment of the worship of the Father or the Spirit but in completion of it. Perfect worship sees the whole Triune God for who He is and what He has done.

We will have new reasons to worship. I love this idea. Andy Davis writes about it at length in His book "Glory Now Revealed." Think back to a moment in your life when God intervened. This may be your salvation, a car wreck you avoided, or the birth of your child. All you know of that experience is what you saw and heard. Imagine sitting down with God and hearing all that He saw and heart. Imagine hearing from Him all He orchestrated to make sure these things happened exactly how they were supposed to. More and more reasons to worship God will forever flow from the throne as we receive an eternal education in what He has done for our good and His glory.

Take some time to consider what song you will sing in His presence? What offering of worship will you bring to Him on that sacred day? What a wonderful moment I experienced in my office as I contemplated this question. What words could I form to express it all? Would I cry out, "Holy, Holy, Holy" with the angels in Isaiah? Would I sing, "Victory in Jesus?" Or would I sing the old hymn that says,

Oh, that day when freed from sinning
I shall see Thy lovely face
Clothed then in blood washed linen
How I'll sing Thy sovereign grace
Come my Lord, no longer tarry
Take my ransomed soul away
Send Thine angels now to carry
Me to realms of endless days
Come Thou Fount of Every Blessing

by Robert Robinson

For Further Study

Each of these chapters contains one of the worship services
that John sees in the book of Revelation.
Worship along with all of creation as you read.

Read Revelation 5

Read Revelation 7

Read Revelation 12

Read Revelation 15

DISCUSSION QUESTIONS

1. How have these chapters helped you understand Heaven?

2. What questions do you still have about Heaven?

3. Why is Jesus the only worthy one to open the scroll from the Father?

4. What description of the throne stood out to you?

5. Who do you think the 24 elders are?

6. What do you think the 4 creatures around the throne represent?

7. What is the focus of the worship of Heaven?

CHAPTER 9

THE NEW HEAVEN AND EARTH

Then I saw a new heaven and a new earth, for the first heaven and the first earth had passed away, and the sea was no more.

Revelation 21:1

Why a new Heaven and New Earth? At this point in the process, is this really necessary? God has already purged the earth of evil. He has already saved His people for all of eternity. Jesus has already been reigning on the earth. There is already a perfect heaven and a restored people on earth. Why are all things new?

I cannot explain the mind of God, but I do want to point out that this idea did not come out of nowhere. It is deeply rooted in the Old Testament. Psalm 97 describes God as one who can melt the mountains. "Fire goes before him and burns up his adversaries all around. His lightning lights up the world; the earth sees and trembles. The mountains melt like wax before the Lord, before the Lord of all the earth." Isaiah 40, where John the Baptist's theology came from, describes God's coming this way: "A voice cries In the wilderness prepare the way of the Lord; make straight in the desert a highway for our God. Every valley shall be lifted up, and every mountain and hill be made low; the uneven ground shall become level, and the rough places a plain. And the glory of the Lord shall be revealed, and all flesh shall see it together, for the mouth of the Lord has spoken."Later in Isaiah, the new heaven and earth are promised by God. "For behold, I create new heavens and a new earth, and the former things shall not be remembered or come into mind. But be glad and rejoice forever in that which I create; for behold, I create Jerusalem to be a joy, and her people to be a gladness."

Ever since the Fall, there has been a need for a new heaven and a new earth. When sin entered into the world, it was broken, and it would not be fixed without the hand of God. Think about the natural world we live in and the brokenness that exists. In 1931, floods in China took the lives of 4,000,000 people. In 1976, an earthquake killed 655,000. Just this year, there have been numerous floods, earthquakes, hurricanes, and tornados, all claiming the lives of people. This world is broken.

Think about it in another light. So much of our world is uninhabitable. 71% of our earth is covered by water. Of what little land is here, it is said that 57% of it is completely uninhabitable. There is a place called Snake Island in Brazil. On the island, 4,000 venomous vipers live. This means there is one snack per square meter there. It is so dangerous to go there that the nation has declared it off-limits.

Another example exists in Centralia, Pennsylvania. In 1962, a fire was started in a mine, and it has been burning ever since. It is releasing poisonous gasses into the air day and night. In 1984, the United States government closed the town down altogether. Thousands of years of sin have not only wrecked us, but it has wrecked our world. We are a long way away from the Garden of Eden.

The new start is not only clearly needed as we observe the world around us, but it was also an idea all the way back in Genesis 6:5-7; 11-13:

Now the earth was corrupt in God's sight, and the earth was filled with violence. And God saw the earth, and behold, it was corrupt, for all flesh had corrupted their way on the earth. And God said to Noah, "I have determined to make an end of all flesh, for the earth is filled with violence through them. Behold, I will destroy them with the earth."

Genesis 6:11-13, ESV

In God's incredible patience and grace, God did not utterly destroy the earth. For the sake of one righteous man, Noah, and his family, did He spare creation. And because of One Righteous Man, Jesus, and His family, the Church, His Bride, God is going to bring down a new heaven and a new earth. Every ounce of the created order will be set right again.

This leads to the natural next questions of "When?" and "What do we do until then?" The answer is found in Mark 13. Jesus tells His disciples to watch and pray. As you drive around your town, the chances are you have passed a bright orange sign telling you to take a detour. It's funny that something so large and in-your-face eventually goes unseen. The sign that far too many people have trouble seeing is the one that says, "Left lane closed. Merge right." Either they don't see it, or they don't believe it. In this text, Jesus is going to lay out a road map for us and show us a series of signs that we will see before arriving where we're going. He will say to take heed, watch, and pray: for Jesus will surely come again.

Jesus has left the temple and will not return. Similar to what happens in Ezekiel 10, the glory of God has left the temple, and judgment is upon it. This chapter alone has caused many theological debates over the centuries (none of which will be settled in this chapter alone). Godly men have disagreed on the details of what is said and whether the events were distant or near future from that moment. I'll address some of these issues along the way, but our goal in this chapter isn't to argue the debatable points but to hear the clear call of Christ. While we may disagree on the full interpretation of this passage, one thing we cannot disagree on is the main point presented by the text: Take heed, watch, and pray: for Jesus will surely come again.

And as he came out of the temple, one of his disciples said to him, "Look, Teacher, what wonderful stones and what wonderful buildings!" And Jesus said to him, "Do you see these great buildings? There will not be left here one stone upon another that will not be thrown down." And as he sat on the Mount of Olives opposite the temple, Peter and James and John and Andrew asked him privately, "Tell us, when will these things be, and what will be the sign when all these things are about to be accomplished?" And Jesus began to say to them, "See that no one leads you astray. Many will come in my name, saying, 'I am he!' and they will lead many astray. And when you hear of wars and rumors of wars, do not be alarmed. This must take place, but the end is not yet. For nation will rise against nation, and kingdom against kingdom. There will be earthquakes in various places; there will be famines. These are but the beginning of the birth pains. "But be on your guard. For they will deliver you over to councils, and you will be beaten in synagogues, and you will stand before governors and kings for my sake, to bear witness before them. And the gospel must first be proclaimed to all nations. And when they bring you to trial and deliver you over, do not be anxious beforehand what you are to say, but say whatever is given you in that hour, for it is not you who speak, but the Holy Spirit. And brother will deliver brother over to death, and the father his child, and children will rise against parents and have them put to death. And you will be hated by all for my name's sake. But the one who endures to the end will be saved.

Mark 13:1-13, ESV

The view from the Mount of Olives is incredible. If you were to stand there now, you could see the Kidron Valley running between you and the temple mount. Sadly, where the temple used to stand is a golden-domed mosque. But when the disciples were following Jesus, asking about the temple, it was a sight to behold. King Herod had this massive temple under construction at the time. It was a 35-acre enclosure that would accommodate 12 football fields. At its highest point, it was 15 stories tall. Can you imagine such a wonder? How much greater of a wonder would it be to see this massive building come crumbling down?

That's what Jesus predicts on the Mount of Olives and introduces the phrase "these things." When will "these things" happen? Jesus gives a list of warning signs. Some signs are worldwide, while others will be specific to God's people.

First, he says that there are signs in the World (Mark 13:5-8). A quick look at world history will show that all of these signs did indeed happen. The False Messiahs have come and gone. One of them was named Theudas. He did his damage during AD 45. The rumors of wars happened during the reign of Caligula in AD 40. He attempted to erect a statue of himself in the temple, which almost caused a war. There were wars. One of them was the Zealot Revolt in AD 66. There have been earthquakes. One was in Phrygia in AD 61, and one was in Pompeii in AD 63. There have been famines, just as Jesus predicted. There were some during the reign of Claudius Caesar in AD 41, 42, 50, 52. Just as Jesus said, all of these things took place.

Second, He said that there would be signs in the Church (Mark 13: 9-13). You need only look at the book of Acts to find these all fulfilled as well. The disciples were put on trial in Acts 5:27-42. They were beaten in synagogues in Acts 18:17. They had to stand before governors and kings in Acts 25. And the Gospel proclaimed to all nations in Acts 2;8; 13-28.

Some godly men have determined that this sign hasn't taken place yet. Therefore, Jesus wasn't speaking about the temple destruction in AD 70 but about the ultimate end of time. However, I think a reasonable argument is that the gospel has gone out to all nations in a sense.

It went to Jerusalem according to Acts 2:5: "Now there were dwelling in Jerusalem Jews, devout men from every nation under heaven." It went to Judea and Samaria according to Acts 8:1: "And there arose on that day a great persecution against the church in Jerusalem, and they were all scattered throughout the regions of Judea and Samaria, except the apostles. And it went to the end of the Earth according to Acts 13-28 and Colossians 1:23 - "if indeed you continue in the faith, stable and steadfast, not shifting from the hope of the gospel that you heard, which has been proclaimed in all creation under heaven, and of which I, Paul, became a minister."

The third sign was Family Against Family. This is happening today and has happened all throughout history. Sadly, family conflict is not a new problem. But it did happen as early as in the family Tacitus in AD 64. If you do the research, you'll see his house was divided over the validity of Jesus. Just as Jesus said, all of these things took place. Finally, we have one more sign to consider.

"From the fig tree learn its lesson: as soon as its branch becomes tender and puts out its leaves, you know that summer is near. So also, when you see these things taking place, you know that he is near, at the very gates. Truly, I say to you, this generation will not pass away until all these things take place. Heaven and earth will pass away, but my words will not pass away.

Mark 13:28-31, ESV

There is debate about whether this sign is related to the AD 70 destruction of the temple or the end of time. Because He is bringing back up the "fig tree" (which was clearly in reference to the temple) and because He uses the phrase "these things" again, I believe this is the final sign/ promise related to the temple's destruction. "This generation will not pass away until these things take place."

Jesus was preaching this sermon around AD 33, and the temple was destroyed in AD 70, confirming even that sign. All of these things were just signs that were to come before "these things' ' also known as the destruction of the temple. In AD 70, Jesus' prediction came true, and the temple in Jerusalem was leveled. Josephus "Caesar ordered the whole city and the temple to be [demolished] to the ground . . . all the rest of the wall encompassing the city was so completely leveled to the ground was to leave future visitors to the spot no ground for believing that it had ever been inhabited."

In a beautiful, miraculous, prophetic, and sovereign way, Jesus' words regarding the temple did not " pass away" but came to be true. This is significant to notice because the prophecy and promise of Jesus are just going to get grander. If He wasn't right on these points, then we have no hope in the remaining ones.

The End in "Those Days" (v. 14-27; 32-37)

"But when you see the abomination of desolation standing where he ought not to be (let the reader understand), then let those who are in Judea flee to the mountains. Let the one who is on the housetop not go down, nor enter his house, to take anything out, and let the one who is in the field not turn back to take his cloak. And alas for women who are pregnant and for those who are nursing infants in those days! Pray that it may not happen in winter. For in those days, there will be such tribulation as has not been from the beginning of the creation that God created until now, and never will be. And if the Lord had not cut short the days, no human being would be saved. But for the sake of the elect, whom he chose, he shortened the days. And then if anyone says to you, 'Look, here is Christ!' or 'Look, there he is!' do not believe it. For false Christs and false prophets will arise and perform signs and wonders, to lead astray, if possible, the elect. But be on guard; I have told you all things beforehand. "But in those days, after

In the first section, the defining term was "these things" in regard to the destruction of the temple. In these sections, you'll notice a shift in the grandeur of the signs and a change to the phrase "in those days." This is one of the reasons I believe Jesus is discussing two separate events in this passage. The first one is a picture of or precursor to the second. Like last time, there are some road signs on the way to the destination.

The first sign of Jesus' return is the Abomination of Desolation (Mark 13:14-18). If you have spent any time studying the book of Daniel, then this language will sound familiar to you. In Daniel, this title was reserved for the man who would defile the temple and end the daily sacrifices that took place.

Jesus is taking this figure of old and applying it to the end times. He is saying there is a person who is going to cause such trouble that it will cause people to flee to the mountains! 2 Thessalonians 2 describes such a man: "Let no one deceive you in any way. For that day will not come unless the rebellion comes first, and the man of lawlessness is revealed, the son of destruction, who opposes and exalts himself against every so-called god or object of worship so that he takes his seat in the temple of God, proclaiming himself to be God." This man will give way to a great tribulation.

The great tribulation is the second sign of Jesus' return Mark 13:19-23. An astounding statement is made: "an affliction that is greater than the world has ever seen and the world will ever see." Greater than the flooding of the earth. Greater than the 10 plagues in Egypt. Greater than the earth opening up to swallow unfaithful members of Israel. Revelation 16 describes this great tribulation as seven bowls of wrath being poured out on the world for its open rebellion. And if you thought it couldn't be more fearsome, hear the final sign:

There will be a cosmic catastrophe (Mark 13:24-25). There are moments when I'm driving down the road, and the sky will have an eerie glow that makes me think of these verses.

Can you imagine a moment when the very light of the world ceases to shine, and its reflection is gone from the moon? The whole world at this moment, whether day or night, will know that the time has come. And just as the sun is quenched, the Son of God will descend.

JESUS' RETURN

And then they will see the Son of Man coming in clouds with great power and glory. And then he will send out the angels and gather his elect from the four winds, from the ends of the earth to the ends of heaven.

Mark 13:26-27, ESV

Jesus comes back, and He saves His people! Praise God that this is how it all ends. All the road signs have been saying, "No outlet; No U-turn; Bridge out." And just as the car meets the cliff, wings burst forth, and we take flight to meet our Savior face to face!

What a glorious future for us! That wonderful day's glory will outshine all the dark moments leading up to it. Just thinking of it now causes my heart to cry out, "Come quickly, Lord Jesus!" God, in His abundant patience, has waited over 2000 since the promise was given on the Mount of Olives. And only the Father knows how much longer it will be until He sends His Son back. So what do we do in the meantime?

There's a temptation to try to break the code of the second coming and pinpoint exactly when and how it will all take place. There's a temptation to build a bomb shelter and prepare for doom's day. There's even a temptation to ignore the second coming altogether. The command given to the disciples as they awaited the destruction of the temple is the same command given to us as we await the Son's return: Take heed: watch and pray.

On Earth As It Is In Heaven

"But concerning that day or that hour, no one knows, not even the angels in heaven, nor the Son, but only the Father. Be on guard, keep awake. For you do not know when the time will come. It is like a man going on a journey, when he leaves home and puts his servants in charge, each with his work, and commands the doorkeeper to stay awake. Therefore stay awake—for you do not know when the master of the house will come, in the evening, or at midnight, or when the rooster crows, or in the morning— lest he come suddenly and find you asleep. And what I say to you I say to all: Stay awake."

Mark 13:32-37, ESV

Jesus uses an illustration to explain the command to watch. He likens the Christian to a porter or gatekeeper. The porter has one job: watch for the master's return. His eyes aren't supposed to leave the horizon. Even at night, he's looking for a glimmer from the torchlight.

Imagine for a moment that you're a standing guard at the gate. Out before you is a long dirt path that leads over the hill. It's nighttime when you hear the sounds of far-off talking, and flecks of light begin to peek over the hill. You stand up and strain your eyes to try to see who is coming. Obviously, you cannot see their faces or make out their voices, so what do you do?

You look for signs that it's your master. You look for a banner leading the way. And if that banner is not there, you alert the city. War is coming!

Depending on who you see coming, it's your job to raise the alarm: whether for welcome or war. Friend, are you raising the alarm? Are you warning them of the danger they are facing?

Are you encouraging your brothers and sisters to fight against the enemy? Are you reminding others to have hope because the master is coming soon? Tragically, many of us are not raising the alarm because we're not watching.

Dear Christian, when was the last time your eyes were on the horizon? When you watch the news, do you fall into despair, anger, or fear? Or does your heart long for Jesus to come back? When you make financial plans, do you consider His return? When you're having yet another conversation with a lost friend/family member, does the closeness of His return weigh on your heart? Friend, the return of Jesus should grip our hearts as tightly as His death and resurrection. It should affect every area of our lives. And it will if we will be watchful. Take heed, watch, and pray: for Jesus will surely come again.

Dear friend, the reality of Jesus' return is one of the greatest hopes for all those who believe in Him. But for those who have not trusted in Him, His return will be your greatest fear realized. When He comes again, He will not be a meek and mild baby in a manger but a warrior king. He will come in a victory march. Repent of your sins and place your faith in Him today, and you'll be invited to march alongside Him. Refuse, and you will share the fate of His enemies: banishment from His kingdom and eternal torment in Hell.

For Further Study

Read Genesis 6

Read Exodus 32

Read Isaiah 65:17-25

Read Isaiah 2:1-5

DISCUSSION QUESTIONS

1. Why does God promise to create a new heaven and earth?

2. Will God's primary dwelling remain in the new heaven?

3. Where will the angels reside in this new era of time?

4. Where will believers reside in this new era of time?

5. What do you think will be different about the new heaven?

6. What do you think will be different about the new earth?

7. What do you hope remains the same about the new earth?

CHAPTER 10

THE NEW JERUSALEM

To put this all into context: Jerusalem on the old earth was the capital city of God's people and the place where the Temple was built. It was the heart of God's nation, Israel. This is not a random city that God has re-created. We're talking about the primary place for God's people to worship God.

It is a place to dwell with God.

And I heard a loud voice from the throne saying, "Behold, the dwelling place of God is with man. He will dwell with them, and they will be his people, and God himself will be with them as their God.

Revelation 21:3, ESV

What was once confined to the holy of holies, which was a 17-foot by 17-foot room, has now been extended to a city. And this was no ordinarily sized city. Even the largest cities in existence today pale in comparison to the size of New Jerusalem. The dimensions of the city that is defined in (Revelation 21:15-17) There, you will read that the city is measured by an angelic rod that measures in stadia. A stadium is equivalent to 607 feet. The length and width of the New Jerusalem is 12,000 stadia. If you do the math, you'll find that that equals roughly 1,380 miles. To put that into perspective, that would be like driving from Charlotte, North Carolina, to San Antonio, Texas. This may be a literal thing where all of God's people will be housed inside the city, or it may mean that God will simply dwell among His people or something in between. But the point being made here is that in the new earth, the glory of God will no longer be contained.

It is a place without the effects of sin.

He will wipe away every tear from their eyes, and death shall be no more, neither shall there be mourning, nor crying, nor pain anymore, for the former things have passed away.

Revelation 21:4, ESV

The first recorded tears from Hagar (Genesis 21:16), and all the ones that follow will be wiped away. The curse of sin that came through Adam will be broken by one man, Jesus.

It is a place made for God's people.

And he who was seated on the throne said, "Behold, I am making all things new." Also, he said, "Write this down, for these words are trustworthy and true." And he said to me, "It is done! I am the Alpha and the Omega, the beginning and the end. To the thirsty, I will give from the spring of the water of life without payment. The one who conquers will have this heritage, and I will be his God, and he will be my son. But as for the cowardly, the faithless, the detestable, as for murderers, the sexually immoral, sorcerers, idolaters, and all liars, their portion will be in the lake that burns with fire and sulfur, which is the second death."

Revelation 21:5-8, ESV

Relish this through Church. When all things are made new, there will not be any rapists, mass murderers, attempts at genocide, or world wars. No evil and no evil people will remain. This new Jerusalem is a place for God's people.

It is a place of indescribable beauty.

Then came one of the seven angels who had the seven bowls full of the seven last plagues and spoke to me, saying, "Come, I will show you the Bride, the wife of the Lamb." And he carried me

The gates and the foundations of the city are not just beautiful but are representative of the foundation of God's people. The 12 gates represent the 12 tribes of Israel. The 12 foundations of the walls represent the 12 apostles. Remember the 24 elders?

Notice the streets of gold as described here (Revelation 21:21). It was like gold but transparent glass - all of the new Jerusalem is essentially transparent, made to reflect and show the brilliance of light.

It is a place of Light.

And I saw no temple in the city, for its temple is the Lord God the Almighty and the Lamb. And the city has no need of sun or moon to shine on it, for the glory of God gives it light, and its lamp is the Lamb. By its light will the nations walk, and the kings of the earth will bring their glory into it, and its gates will never be shut by day—and there will be no night there. They will bring into it the glory and the honor of the nations. But nothing unclean will ever enter it, nor anyone who does what is detestable or false, but only those who are written in the Lamb's book of life.

Revelation 21:22-27, ESV

A place of brilliant light. Like the throne room of chapter 4, but expanded to encompass a city, and not just a city, but a city the size of nations. And it will reflect all of the goodness of God, down to the goodness of God displayed in the many nations (Revelation 21:26). The best of every nation will remain because God worked it out in us while it existed. Our imaginations can run wild with what all that might include. I sure hope sports make the cut.

It is a place like Eden (v. 1-5)

Then the angel showed me the river of the water of life, bright as crystal, flowing from the throne of God and of the Lamb through the middle of the street of the city; also, on either side of the river, the tree of life with its twelve kinds of fruit, yielding its fruit each month. The leaves of the tree were for the healing of the nations. No longer will there be anything accursed, but the throne of God and of the Lamb will be in it, and his servants will worship him. They will see his face, and his name will be on their foreheads. And night will be no more. They will need no light of lamp or sun, for the Lord God will be their light, and they will reign forever and ever.

Revelation 22:1-5, ESV

In the beginning, God created the heavens and the earth. And on the earth, he created a garden where He intended to dwell with man and give them dominion over everything under His authority. And in the end, God creates a new heaven and a new earth. He plants His people back in the garden city of the New Jerusalem, and they are to have dominion over everything under His authority. Every problem created by man in Genesis 3 is completely and utterly restored in Revelation 22. And I love how this section ends (Revelation 21:6-7).

ON EARTH AS IT IS IN HEAVEN

The glories of the New Jerusalem, our forever home, are impossible to deny. Meditation on that wonderful destination would benefit your soul. Take time to attempt to draw what is described in these chapters. Do the research it takes to find all of the colors of the precious stones that are used. In whatever way you can, create some kind of rendering of this place.

As you do this, it will cause your soul to long all the more for home. And you'll grow increasingly thankful for what God has prepared for you. You'll grow all the more aware of just how little you deserve such a gift. And in the end, you'll grow all the more worshipful of your God and King.

For Further Study

Read Revelation 21

Read Revelation 22

Read Genesis 2

Read Genesis 21:8-20

Discussion Questions

1. What is significant that God will dwell in New Jerusalem?

2. How would you describe the new city?

3. Why do you think the stones are all translucent?

4. Why does God describe Himself as the Light of the city?

5. What is the significance of the similarities between the New Jerusalem and the Garden of Eden?

6. Do you think the tree of the knowledge of good and evil will be in the New Jerusalem?

7. What do you look forward to the most about New Jerusalem?

CHAPTER 11

THE NEW BODIES

I'm starting to fall apart. Each morning, I wake up to shoulder pain. When I go for my morning jog, my right foot aches. Throughout the days, these two ailments shoot pain through my body. These are clear signs that my body is breaking down. But more than those things, my new need for glasses has opened my eyes to my age.

For years, I have known that I need glasses. As I've gotten older, it has become increasingly difficult for me to read road signs as I'm driving. My nearsighted vision was weakening. I finally decided to go to the doctor to see what suggestions they may have for me.

As I walked into the building, I assumed it would be a quick visit. I expected them to say that I may need a pair of glasses for driving, but my vision is fine overall. Halfway through the tour of fuzzy letters, I began to realize that my vision was worse than I thought. Finally, it was time for them to begin finding the right lens prescription to correct my vision. I flew through a series of lenses that slightly increased or decreased the blurriness of the letters until the doctor eventually said, "Okay, this is your vision without glasses." It was a blurry mess.

"And this is your vision with glasses." That moment of clarity was overwhelming. I was so filled with joy that I laughed. Going on the emotional roller coaster of realizing just how broken my sight was to just how good it could be brought me to a moment of praise and longing for Heaven.

As I sat in the waiting room while my eyes adjusted and the doctors figured out the paperwork, I stared at a blurry street sign. I sat and thought about the wonderful gift of glasses. And then I marveled at my wonderful home in Heaven. You see, there won't be any need for glasses in the presence of God. And glasses are just the tip of the iceberg. One day, all of the little and big things that are wrong in our bodies and this world will be fixed. Everything from cancer to cataracts will be removed and replaced with God's original design for life. Perfect life in His presence. Can you imagine all of the wonderful things we're missing out on? If beautiful colors and incredible sights take our breath away now, how much more when we really see them as they were intended? Oh, what a paradise awaits God's people!

These bodies don't last forever. What if I told you they weren't designed that way? What if I told you that all the aches and pains, the slow decay, it was all because of sin?

In our time together tonight, we're going to think about the new/glorified bodies that we will receive. Our glorified bodies are given to glorify God.

We've covered a lot of ground in this book so far. We discussed Heaven as it is now and it's perfect worship. We've discussed the New Heaven, New Earth, and the New Jerusalem to come, streets of gold and all. In our study of what our glorified bodies are, we want to stick as closely to what we know for sure, but there will be a few inferences along the way. But let's at least start with the concrete promise of Scripture that glorified bodies are promised.

THE PROMISE

But our citizenship is in heaven, and from it we await a Savior, the Lord Jesus Christ, who will transform our lowly body to be like his glorious body, by the power that enables him even to subject all things to himself.

Philippians 3:20-21, ESV

Let's break down the key phrase in these verses: "who will transform our lowly body to be like his glorious body." In some translations of the Bible, it says our "vile body." The word vile there can be misleading. We understand vile to be disgusting or off-putting, but the Greek word doesn't mean that. The Greek word means low or humble. According to this passage, our bodies are slow in comparison to the body to come. We should have no problem accepting that our bodies are lowly. Look at how frail they are and how short of a lifespan they endure. In comparison to perfect eternity, they are very low.

Notice what will happen to our lowly body next: it will be transformed and be like another. These two phrases are very important. Our lowly bodies are not said to be destroyed and done away with. They are going to be transformed. The promise of 1 Thessalonians 4 is that when Jesus returns, the dead in Christ will rise. Their bodies will not be forgotten or dismissed. Their bodies will be changed.

But transformed how? They will be like each other. This word is used only one other time in the New Testament, and it speaks of how we are to be conformed to the image of Jesus in our lives. Like pressing clay into a mold, our bodies will be fashioned. So, we have to ask, fashioned into what? The answer is Jesus' body.

1 John 3:2 says it like this, "Beloved, we are God's children now, and what we will be has not yet appeared; but we know that when he appears we shall be like him, because we shall see him as he is." This does not mean that we will all become clones of Jesus, but our bodies will resemble the essence of His body. The unique qualities of the resurrected body of Jesus will be found in our bodies as well. So, with this promise in mind, let's get into the details that Scripture provides. If we're promised a glorified body that mirrors the body of Christ, what does that look like?

THE DETAILS

So is it with the resurrection of the dead. What is sown is perishable; what is raised is imperishable. It is sown in dishonor; it is raised in glory. It is sown in weakness; it is raised in power. It is sown a natural body; it is raised a spiritual body. If there is a natural

body, there is also a spiritual body. Thus it is written, "The first man Adam became a living being"; the last Adam became a life-giving spirit. But it is not the spiritual that is first but the natural, and then the spiritual. The first man was from the earth, a man of dust; the second man is from heaven. As was the man of dust, so also are those who are of the dust, and as is the man of heaven, so also are those who are of heaven. Just as we have borne the image of the man of dust, we shall also bear the image of the man of heaven.

1 Corinthians 15:42-29, ESV

Verse 35 of this chapter asks the question we are seeking answers to: "How are the dead raised up? and with what body do they come?" Paul uses an agriculture analogy to explain the change that takes place in the resurrection (1 Corinthians 15:37-38). This is a strange analogy, but go with me for a minute.

Paul says our bodies are like seeds planted in the ground. When you plant something, you don't expect that seed to be the product. You expect a change to happen and something to grow in its place. This is what he says the resurrection of our glorified bodies will be like: what was laid to rest will be different from what emerges. What are the differences?

Paul says that our glorified bodies will be imperishable or incorruptible. I love this word here because it gets to the heart of the issue. Sin is corruption. It brought death to the world. It is the reason there needed to be a change, to begin with. But our glorified bodies will be incorruptible. This means that they will not suffer the curse of sin, which is death. They won't break down. There will be no need for glasses, slings, or wheelchairs. And they will not suffer the control of sin and endure its temptation. Just like the old song says, "all the ransomed ones of God will be saved to sin no more." All physical and spiritual frustration and pain that we endure will be no more.

Paul also says that our glorified bodies will be glorified. The word glory can have different meanings based on its context, so let's highlight the opposite of what is meant by glory: dishonor.

Almost to mirror the concept of corruption, dishonor sheds light on the view of a dead body. People can die for honorable reasons, like fighting for our country. First responders lose their lives while trying to save others. Even Jesus died for other people on His cross.

Paul isn't saying all death is dishonorable. He is saying that a dead body by itself is not honorable. Specifically for the Jewish people, it was something to be avoided because it was considered unclean. The resurrected glorified body will be one of honor and glory because it will be raised in the way that God had intended it to be. Without the effect of sin present in and on it.

Next, Paul teaches that our glorified bodies will be powerful. What once was weak and lifeless will be filled with vitality again. Strength will refill our muscles, and breath will inflate our lungs. There will be power yet again in our glorified bodies.

Then Paul says that our glorified bodies will be spiritual. At first glance, you may read this and think that our bodies will be spirit. But that's not what it says. It says, "The natural body was sown, and a spiritual body was raised." Paul explains in verses 45-49 that our resurrected bodies are where two Adams collide. In the first Adam of Genesis, we have the physical, natural body. In the second Adam, Jesus, we have the spiritual body. Jesus says of Himself that he is the resurrection and the life. These two realities will come together in perfect unity in our glorified bodies.

What exactly that means has been hard for me to put my finger on, but here's what I've gathered so far. Right now, there is a separation between body and soul. "To be absent from the body is present with the Lord." Then, there will be no separation but perfect unity between body and soul. Our glorified bodies will be so perfectly unified with the ransomed soul that the best way to describe it would be to call it a "spiritual body."

These verses take place after the resurrection of Christ. This glorified body that He now has is that ours will mirror according to the other passages that we have studied. This passage shows us that our glorified bodies will be recognizable. If so much changes in the resurrection, it has to be asked whether or not we will recognize one another? For anyone who has lost a child, will their body be full grown? For those who have died at an old age, will their body be useful?

I don't know the answers to these questions, but one thing is clear. We will recognize one another.

Not only is Jesus recognized here, but he is recognized over and over again by various groups of people, according to 1 Corinthians 15. And not only Jesus but think of who Jesus met with on the Mount of Transfiguration. Pop Quiz: Who were they? The answer is Moses and Elijah. How do we know this? Because they were recognizable, even to the disciples who had never seen them physically before.

Just for further confirmation, think of the parable of Lazarus and the rich man. The rich man who knew Lazarus as a poor beggar saw him from Hell and recognized him in Heaven. This is a clear teaching that however old or young our bodies will be when we are resurrected, we will recognize one another. Not only are they recognizable according to this passage, but they are clearly physical as well.

As we see Jesus interact with His followers, it is clear that His and our glorified bodies will be physical. Two things happen here that prove the physical nature of the resurrected body. The first is that there is physical touch. They were able to see and touch his scars. Famously, in John 20, Thomas is known for doubting up until the point he can touch Him. His glorified body, as well as ours, was still physical.

The second is that his body had physical desires. I was tempted to use the word needs here, but I'm not sure that is quite right. I don't know that our bodies will need food and water like they do now, but they will enjoy it. Jesus eats a fish breakfast with His disciples on the beach.

Many times, Heaven is described as a place where a feast is taking place. It says in Isaiah 25 that God will swallow up death forever and lay for His people a great feast, "On this mountain, the Lord of hosts will make for all peoples a feast of rich food, a feast of well-aged wine, of rich food full of marrow, of aged wine well refined." I don't know what all will be on the menu of Heaven, but we will physically enjoy every last bite.

While these things are wonderfully true of our new bodies to come, there are some differences between ours and Christ's. There are two supernatural things that Jesus does in His resurrected body that we shouldn't expect. The first is His ability to conceal His identity.

That very day two of them were going to a village named Emmaus, about seven miles from Jerusalem, and they were talking with each other about all these things that had happened. While they were talking and discussing together, Jesus himself drew near and went with them. But their eyes were kept from recognizing him.

Luke 24:13-16, ESV

Jesus did this many times during the 40 days He remained on earth before ascending. He did this with different purposes in mind, but we should not expect to do this: nor would there be much use for us to do this anyway. The second supernatural ability of Christ that we should not expect is teleportation.

So they drew near to the village to which they were going. He acted as if he were going farther, but they urged him strongly, saying, "Stay with us, for it is toward evening and the day is now far spent." So he went in to stay with them. When he was at table with them, he took the bread and blessed and broke it and gave it to them. And their eyes were opened, and they recognized him. And he vanished from their sight.

Luke 24:28-31, ESV

Once again, Jesus did this many times with His disciples where He would appear among them, or disappear. That would be an awesome ability but one we should not expect. Remember, Jesus is God. He could have and always will be able to do things we cannot. Sorry to burst any dreams of being a superhero.

My son has some issues with his liver, and annually, we have to take a trip to a children's hospital in a large city far away to do a check-up. I hate making that trip. And I know he has to hate it, too. Each time, he has to endure the long drive. They press on his belly and draw blood. We have to wait anxiously for the results that sound like a foreign language when we read them. Doctors' visits of any kind are just difficult.

Friend, there will be no need for doctor visits in Heaven. No tests to be run. No results to wait on. No ailments to treat. Good is good, church. Far better to us than we could ever deserve. And we will experience that goodness in every fashion imaginable for all of eternity.

On Earth, As It Is In Heaven - Take Care of Your Body

The promise of new, glorified bodies to come should not tempt us toward disparaging our current bodies. Although God can and will redeem our bodies, no matter the state they die in, it would be bad stewardship of them to destroy unnecessarily. Paul even speaks to Timothy about having a proper view of our body in light of eternity.

Have nothing to do with irreverent, silly myths. Rather train yourself for godliness; 8 for while bodily training is of some value, godliness is of value in every way, as it holds promise for the present life and also for the life to come.

2 Timothy 4:7-8, ESV

Our primary goal in this life and in preparation for the next is to pursue godliness. But even Paul will not deny that bold training is of some value. It is worth our time and effort to try to take care of our bodies. If our flesh and bones are what God formed in our mother's wombs and what He will raise again one day, it makes sense to take care of them. What are you doing to protect the gift of your body that God has given you?

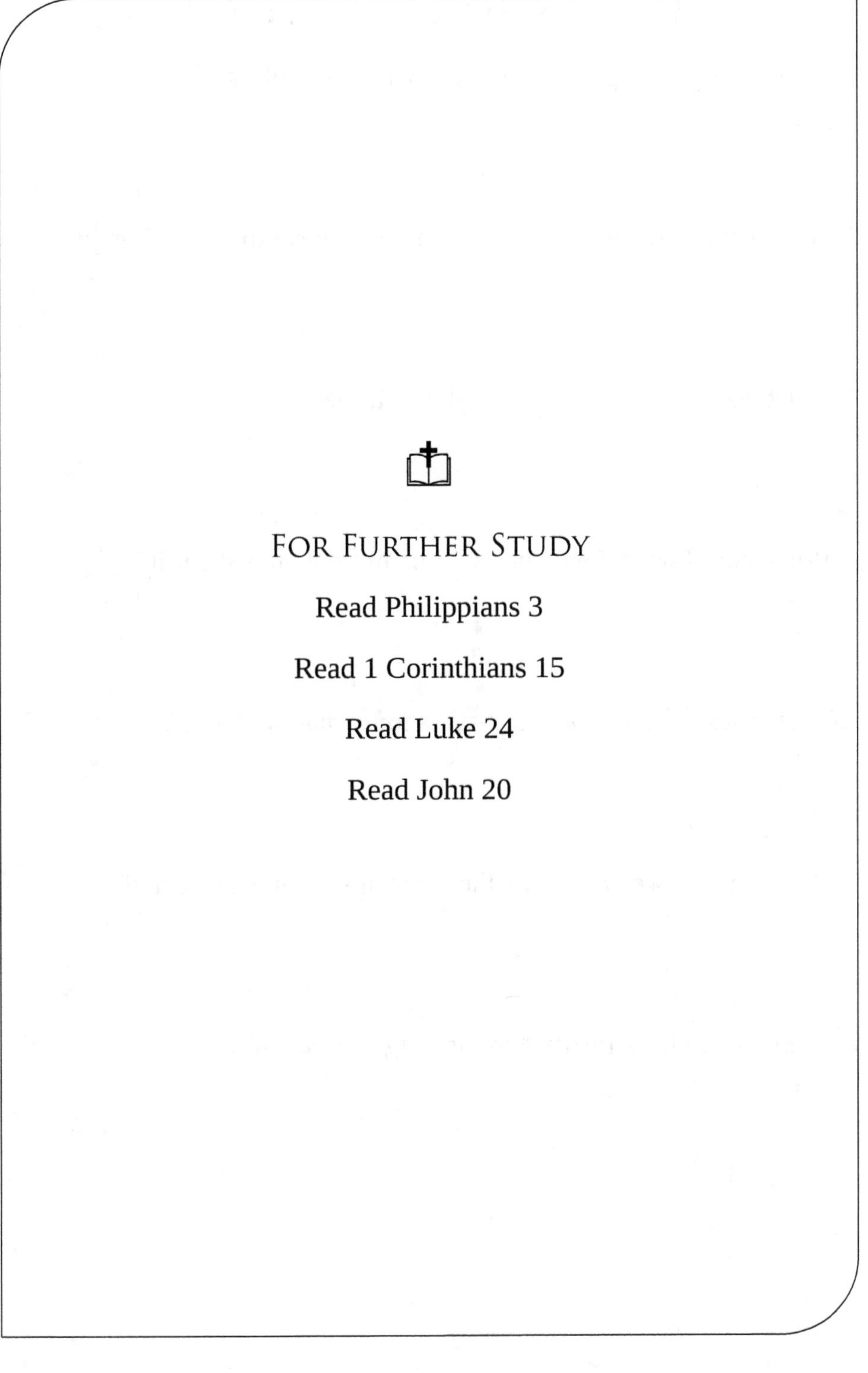

For Further Study

Read Philippians 3

Read 1 Corinthians 15

Read Luke 24

Read John 20

DISCUSSION QUESTIONS

1. How have you experienced your own body failing?

2. How would life be different if you didn't have those challenges?

3. What do you think our new bodies will be like?

4. Why should we believe they will be more than just spirit?

5. What questions do you still have about what they will be like?

6. Do you think we will all be the same age when resurrected?

7. Who do you look forward to meeting in Heaven?

CHAPTER 12

HELL: THE ANTI-HEAVEN

Heaven is the greatest promise any man could receive. The joys and glory that awaits there are beyond compare to anything this world may offer. From the food that will be served there to the incredible colors and music, there will be nothing but pure bliss for all of eternity for all who place their faith in Jesus. But we must remember that Heaven is a reward. This means that there is an equal and opposite punishment. The sad reality of the Bible is that there is an antithesis to Heaven. It is a place called Hell. It is the opposite of Heaven in many ways.

THE REALITY OF HELL

"Then he will say to those on his left, 'Depart from me, you cursed, into the eternal fire prepared for the devil and his angels. For I was hungry and you gave me no food, I was thirsty and you gave me no drink, I was a stranger and you did not welcome me, naked and you did not clothe me, sick and in prison and you did not visit me.' Then they also will answer, saying, 'Lord, when did we see you hungry or thirsty or a stranger or naked or sick or in prison, and did not minister to you?' Then he will answer them, saying, 'Truly, I say to you, as you did not do it to one of the least of these, you did not do it to me.' And these will go away into eternal punishment, but the righteous into eternal life."

Matthew 25:41-46, ESV

Jesus is describing the day He returns and brings judgment on the earth. He says He will separate the "sheep from the goats." The sheep at His right hand will be welcomed into Heaven forever more. The goats on His left hand will be cast away. Heaven is the home of God, a place prepared for His angels and His people. Hell is the prison of Satan and His demons, prepared for them, and sadly, many men go there too.

Friend, let me be clear here. Not all people go to Heaven. Only those who place their faith in the Biblical Jesus are given that wonderful future. Those who do not go to heaven are not in purgatory, nor are they annihilated, as some teach. They go to Hell forever. There is no doubt in Jesus' teaching or the overall teaching of the Bible that Hell is as real of a place as Heaven.

How does Jesus describe Hell? He uses terms like everlasting fire and everlasting punishment. In the same way that we cannot imagine or describe the glories of Heaven, we dare not imagine the punishment of Hell. While we may not want to linger here too long, it is good for us to have a healthy fear of God and His ability to punish (Matthew 10:28).

GOD IS NOT PRESENT

This is evidence of the righteous judgment of God, that you may be considered worthy of the kingdom of God, for which you are also suffering— since indeed God considers it just to repay with affliction those who afflict you, and to grant relief to you who are afflicted as well as to us, when the Lord Jesus is revealed from heaven with his mighty angels in flaming fire, inflicting vengeance on those who do not know God and on those who do not obey the gospel of our Lord Jesus. They will suffer the punishment of eternal destruction, away from the presence of the Lord and from the glory of his might, when he comes on that day to be glorified in his saints, and to be marveled at among all who have believed, because our testimony to you was believed.

2 Thessalonians 1:5-10, ESV

Paul's description of Hell to the churches in Thessalonica is intense. He says that their punishment will be an affliction that God repays. It will be a place of flaming fire. It will be the infliction of vengeance from God Himself. There will be a suffering of eternal destruction. All of these things ought to strike fear into anyone's heart. But the most devastating judgment found in Hell is that those who are destined there will be taken "away from the presence of God and the glory of His might."

Take in all of what this means. If God is no longer present, then there is no chance for redemption. Our salvation is completely dependent on the work of God. According to Galatians 1:3-5, the Gospel is that "the Lord Jesus Christ . . . gave himself for our sins to deliver us from the present evil age, according to the will of our God and Father, to whom be the glory forever and ever." The gospel is God's plan to free His people from sin by the death and resurrection of His Son to the glory of His name.

What have you contributed to your salvation? Did you make the plan? Did you free yourself? Did you die and rise again? What did you do? Nothing! Absolutely nothing! This is why it is God who gets the glory forever and ever. Amen! Jonathan Edwards famously said, "You contribute nothing to your salvation except the sin that made it necessary."

Therefore, if God's presence is no longer there, then there is no chance of salvation. No matter how sorrowful the heart is in Hell, it will not be saved. There is no amount of repentance or faith that redeemed that wretched soul any longer. There will be no mercy, grace, or forgiveness in Hell. And with God fully departed from that place, the individual will not be able to forgive themselves. Everlasting guilt and agony is the punishment of Hell.

Not only does the removal of God's presence remove all chances of salvation, it removes all that is good. Think about it. Where did joy come from? What about hope? Who is called Love in the Bible? Every good and perfect gift comes down from the Father of lights, says the Book of James. The covenant that God made with Noah secured what theologians call "common grace."

The reason that the righteous and the wicked get rain and sun is because of common grace. The sinner and the saint alike have the benefit of medicine. All people enjoy food and music in this life. We all have experiences of love, joy, and peace. No matter your standing before God, in the end, we all experience these things in some form because of common grace.

The common grace of God is not present in Hell because God is not present. There will be no love, joy, or peace. There will be no heart-warming movies, delicious meals, or satisfying drinks of water. Absolutely no pleasure will be there because the Father of Lights will have nothing to give those who earn this punishment. Words fail to express the absolute horror that Hell will be like.

HELL IS AN ETERNAL PUNISHMENT

Then I saw a great white throne and him who was seated on it. From his presence the earth and sky fled away, and no place was found for them. And I saw the dead, great and small, standing before the throne, and books were opened. Then another book was opened, which is the book of life. And the dead were judged by what was written in the books, according to what they had done. And the sea gave up the dead who were in it, Death and Hades gave up the dead who were in them, and they were judged, each one of them, according to what they had done. Then Death and Hades were thrown into the lake of fire. This is the second death, the lake of fire. And if anyone's name was not found written in the book of life, he was thrown into the lake of fire.

Revelation 20:11-15, ESV

The way Hell is described throughout the Bible could lead someone to believe that it is not an eternal destination. It's called a place of destruction. It has the imagery of fire that burns and gets rid of anything in its path. In the passage above and later in Revelation 21:8, it is called a place of the second death. These images all convey an idea of annihilation.

130

Tragically, this is not the case. The clear teaching of the Bible is that Hell is an eternal place for the eternal punishment of those who reject the Gospel. As we have already read, it is a place of "eternal destruction" (2 Thessalonians 1). That phrase is like an oxymoron. Like jumbo shrimp or bittersweet, it contains two words that seem to contradict each other. And yet, the place called Hell is both eternal and destructive. It will feel like being destroyed for all eternity.

We have also already read in Matthew 25 that it is a place of eternal punishment that is juxtaposed with the joy of eternal life in Hell. The second death will be like an eternal death experience. It will feel like you're being destroyed and are dying for the rest of time. In Jesus' parable in Matthew 13, He describes it this way, "So it will be at the end of the age. The angels will come out and separate the evil from the righteous and throw them into the fiery furnace. In that place there will be weeping and gnashing of teeth."

The phrase gnashing of teeth is supposed to put the picture of grinding your teeth because of intense pain in your mind. Maybe you've stubbed your toe and clinged your teeth together in response to that pain. That kind of response will be what our bodies would experience. But there would be no relief. When you stub your toe or hit your finger with a hammer, eventually, there comes numbness and healing. In Hell, there will be no numb moments. The weeping and gnashing of teeth will never end.

One more eternal reality is told by Jesus in Mark 9. There, He says, "And if your eye causes you to sin, tear it out. It is better for you to enter the kingdom of God with one eye than with two eyes to be thrown into hell, 'where their worm does not die and the fire is not quenched.'" This phrase is intended to draw the reader's mind to a place called Gehenna from biblical days.

There was a valley outside of the city of Jerusalem. This place was essentially the city dump. Instead of a landfill, people would toss all of their trash and refuse into the valley. You can imagine the stench that would have been present in this valley. Far worse than any smell you've experienced at the local dump. For there would have been nothing to contain the smell.

Where there are great amounts of trash, there are flies. Maybe you've gone to empty your own trashcan and found it surrounded by flies. Where do those flies come from? What is their infant state? They start as eggs which hatch into larvae, worm-like creatures. They are white- or cream-colored maggots that squirm and eat as much as they can. It turns my stomach just thinking about it.

Jesus is teaching that Hell, this place of eternal death and destruction, will be filled with the "worm that never dies." Because there is never-ending decay, there is a never-ending presence of a maggot-like creature constantly feasting on the flesh of those present. Along with the worm that never dies in the valley, there is fire as well.

This fire was known far and wide as one that would never die in the valley of Gehenna. Because the trash never stopped flowing in, the fire was always being fueled. Gehenna was a picture of Hell. But it even failed to do it justice. If your mental image of Hell is limited to a valley of fire, you still haven't grasped its gruesome and grotesque nature.

With all of this information before us, at some point, you're going to be tempted to ask the question, "Is this just?" Is it right for God to dole out this level of punishment? Sure, those who do not believe and reject His good Word should not be admitted into Heaven forever. But is it right for them to be thrown into Hell for all of eternity?

HELL IS A JUST PUNISHMENT

When we're tempted to question the justice of God, we must be reminded of the seriousness of the offense of sin. We can be tempted to think that some sins are more or less serious in God's eyes. Calling someone a bad name is not as bad as killing them, right? Stealing one dollar is not as serious of an offense as stealing one million, right?

Our court system certainly operates this way. There are different punishments for different crimes. And the punishment is designed to fit the severity of the crime. And so if someone lives a relatively moral life, although they do not trust in Jesus, surely they don't deserve Hell. That is the logic and the argument of those who question the justice of Hell. Allow me to point your attention to what is taught by James.

To break the law of God or to sin is not as simple as committing a crime. To break any Law of God is to break the very heart of God. The same one who said, "Do not commit adultery," also said, "Do not bear false witness." Each and every sin that we commit is an infraction against God's holy law. This means that each and every sin is an offense to the Law Maker. When we sin, we do not just break a list of arbitrary rules. We rebel against the King of all creation.

This is not to say that different sins should not have different earthly consequences. In the law books of the Old Testament, there are plenty of punishments listed other than eternal destruction in Hell. But there is the same ultimate punishment for all who sin. How is this just?

Consider the offended party. If someone sins against us, we can only expect so much restitution. Because at the end of the day, we are sinners too. Most of the time, when we are sinned against, we have also sinned against that person. None of us are perfect. But this is not true of God. He is perfect.

There is not a single instance in all of eternity that God has ever sinned. With holy perfection, God holds the right to make the Law and submit any person to punishment. A sin against an eternally and infinitely holy God rightly earns an eternal and infinite punishment, no matter how big the sin is. It is not the law alone that was offended by our sin, but a perfectly holy God.

This means that He is just to punish mankind in this way. He has the right as the Judge of all creation to say what a fitting punishment for the crime is. And His justice is not limited to just this facet of thought. He is just in that He treats all people and even angels the same way. If anything goes against Him, there is a just price to pay.

Now I want to remind you, although you once fully knew it, that Jesus, who saved people out of the land of Egypt, afterward destroyed those who did not believe. And the angels who did not stay within their own position of authority, but left their proper dwelling, he has kept in eternal chains under gloomy darkness until the judgment of the great day—just as Sodom and Gomorrah and the surrounding cities, which likewise indulged in sexual immorality and pursued unnatural desire, serve as an example by undergoing a punishment of eternal fire.

Jude 1:5-7, ESV

Jude pulls out the entire Old Testament to defend his case as he references 8 different OT events. We don't have the time to fully examine each of these events, but what we will see is a clear pattern of unbelief among them. Let's begin with the first example in verse 5.

If you're unfamiliar with the story of the Exodus, let me give you the highlights. After watching Pharaoh's army drown in the sea's wake, God began to lead His people to the Promised Land. However, mere days into the journey, the people began a long string of grumbling and murmuring, saying, "God doesn't love us. He can't provide for us out here. We would rather be slaves." The judgment for this unrepentant sin was 40 years of wandering in the wilderness. A whole generation of people would die before they finally made it into the promised land.

Let's see the cycle together: Unbelief - Unrepentance - Undergoing Judgment. That's the cycle that he begins with, and it runs throughout all of his examples. Look back at verse 6. Jude is making reference to an event in Genesis 6 where the angels looked down on earth and lusted after mankind. They did not believe that God's design for them was good enough. They wanted more. So they pursued unrepentant sin before God and had sexual relations with man. This prompted undergoing judgment as God immediately after this event sent a flood, saving only Noah and His family.

Again, we see it in verse 7. The cities of Sodom and Gomorrah were so wicked. They weren't just known for one sin but for all kinds of sins. The pinnacle of this was when Lot allowed His daughter to be sexually abused in order to protect some angels who came to his house. These cities did not believe in God, nor believe He was worth obeying. They lived in constant unrepentance. They underwent the judgment of fire reigning down on the city and destroying it forever. Whether you're a part of God's people, an angel, or a wicked city, when unbelief creeps in, judgment is on its way.

This history of God's justice is proven in Scripture. He will not overlook sin. He will not ignore rebellion. All of creation, whether mankind, false teachers, or angels, are judged by God. And if they are found guilty of sin, then He justly punishes them.

On Earth As It Is In Heaven

This chapter ought to do two things for your soul. It ought to grow your longing for Heaven and stir a fire to save the world from Hell. If you understand the gravity of that kind of eternal destination, you would never wish that on even your worst enemy. And so, I challenge you, friend, to be urgent in your message. Stop reading right now and make a plan. Figure out who you need to talk to. Set a time to text, call, or visit them. Don't wait any longer. Neither you nor your friend is promised tomorrow. But we are promised an eternity somewhere based on our faith. Where will yours be placed?

FOR FURTHER STUDY

Read Matthew 10:26-33

Read Matthew 25:31-46

Read 2 Thessalonians 1:5-12

Read Matthew 13:47-50

DISCUSSION QUESTIONS

1. In what ways is Hell the opposite of Heaven?

2. Is it just that some people go to Hell?

3. How would you describe Hell to someone who has not heard of it?

4. Do you think Hell is an everlasting punishment or an annihilation of unbelievers?

5. Do you think there will be interaction among those in Hell?

6. Is there any hope for those who are in Hell? Why or why not?

7. How does this eternal punishment motivate you today?

CHAPTER 13

COMMON QUESTIONS ABOUT HEAVEN

This book is not exhaustive on the topic of heaven. In fact, it may have raised more questions than it answered in your mind. The primary purpose of the book was to answer the concrete questions that the Bible answers. You should be able to walk away from this book knowing the most important things about Heaven.

Knowing these things, however, does not eliminate the smaller concerns about Heaven. In this chapter, we will take time to address some of the most common questions that are asked about the life to come in our eternal home. As a disclaimer, the answers to these questions are the writer's own opinion. Many of them are not directly addressed in God's Word, so all that can be offered is an educated guess based on the overall teachings of the Bible.

WILL MY PETS BE IN HEAVEN?

If you have a pet, then you know how close they become to your family. For many people, pets are treated just like family. They will receive Christmas presents, birthday parties, and even dress up on Halloween. They have become so close to us that it is common practice to call our pets our "fur babies." They express love and affection and become extremely important to us. So, it makes sense to think about what happens to them when they die. Will they be in Heaven with us?

I want to address this question by asking and answering a related one first. Let's first ask and answer whether or not there are animals in Heaven before we get to our individual pets. There are various Scriptures that give us reason to believe that there are animals in Heaven. In Revelation 6, there are four horsemen who bring great judgment to the earth. We don't have time to go into all of those details, but each of those men is riding a horse. Those horses are all described as a different color in that chapter.

In Isaiah 11, when the day of the Lord is described, and the New Heaven and Earth are in mind, there is an incredible description of animals. There is a promise of harmony between lions and lambs. Leopards and goats are said to lay down with one another. So docile will be the animals that little children will be able to lead all kinds of them (Isaiah 11:6). If the New Earth is like returning to the Garden of Eden, it would make sense that animals are present.

Finally, I wanted to point out to you the description of Jesus at the end of the times from Revelation 19.

Then I saw heaven opened, and behold, a white horse! The one sitting on it is called Faithful and True, and in righteousness he judges and makes war. His eyes are like a flame of fire, and on his head are many diadems, and he has a name written that no one knows but himself. He is clothed in a robe dipped in blood, and the name by which he is called is The Word of God. And the armies of heaven, arrayed in fine linen, white and pure, were following him on white horses. From his mouth comes a sharp sword with which to strike down the nations, and he will rule them with a rod of iron. He will tread the winepress of the fury of the wrath of God the Almighty. On his robe and on his thigh he has a name written, King of kings and Lord of lords.

Revelation 19:11-16, ESV

Jesus and those who accompany Him in His army all ride in on white horses. To be fair, all of this could be an allegory, but with the repeated references in the Old and New Testament, it would be an honest assessment of Scripture to assume that animals will be present in Heaven.

That thought, however, is very different from whether or not our animals will be in Heaven. There is a difference between humanity and all of creation. The Bible says that mankind alone bears the image of God. No other creature is given that distinction. As image bearers, we can know God and have a relationship with Him. We have the capacity not only to recognize our lost and sinful state but to repent and plead the blood of Christ in faith for salvation.

No pets are going to do this. Yes, they have personalities. They have the ability to love and show loyalty. They are aware of who we are and what is going on in the world. But the Bible does not claim that any animal has a soul that must be saved. In this regard, it would be hard for me to confidently say that any of our pets would be in Heaven when we get there.

God is God, and He can do whatever He wants. It may please Him to bring joy to us in that way in Heaven. He may want to bless His people by allowing them to continue that relationship with their pets forever. But it is not a promise that we can hold onto tightly.

If this is hard for you to process, let me remind you of something. The focal point of Heaven is God. He will be your primary concern. And if He is going to be the one who wipes away every tear, then any sorrow you may feel over your former pets will be perfectly comforted by your Savior. Take heart, dear friend. God loves you deeply and will be gracious to you.

WILL WE STILL BE MARRIED?

I love my spouse deeply. Even thinking about their passing makes my stomach drop and my heart race. If we long to see our pets in Heaven, how much more would we hope to see our spouses? Not only to see them but to be united with them in the way that we are now.

If you're married, you have a special relationship with one person that is unique to every other relationship in your life. You're more committed to them than anyone else. All of your life decisions are influenced by them. Most likely, when you think about the end of your life, you have their best interests in mind. So naturally, we want to know if we will be married to that person in Heaven. There are two passages of Scripture that address this pretty clearly.

In this passage, the Sadducees are trying to trip Jesus up with a theological question. In the Law, there is a rule that requires the family of a widow to provide for her. In an extreme circumstance, the Sadducees pose the possibility of a widow having 7 different husbands who all pass away before she does. The question in mind is this, "If someone is married 7 times in their life, who will be their spouse in Heaven?"

It is a ridiculous question designed to poke holes in the concept of resurrection. The Sadducees didn't believe in resurrection. For our purposes, let's just focus on Jesus' answer. He says in no uncertain terms, "For in the resurrection they neither marry nor are given in marriage." Remember that the resurrection in mind is the event that happens before all things are made new. This response doesn't directly answer the question about marriage in Heaven, but it provides all that we need to have a well-informed answer.

If we cannot expect to remain married to enter into a new marriage after the resurrection that is to come, we should not expect marriage to be a factor in Heaven. This in no way means that your spouse will or will not be there. It also does not mean that you won't know or enjoy your relationship with your spouse in Heaven. It does mean that you won't have that commitment to them that you do now. It means that you will relate to them in a different way.

The main reason for this is pretty clear when you think about it: you'll have a higher allegiance and no need for the companionship and security of marriage.

> *Then I heard what seemed to be the voice of a great multitude, like the roar of many waters and like the sound of mighty peals of thunder, crying out, "Hallelujah! For the Lord our God the Almighty reigns. Let us rejoice and exult and give him the glory, for the marriage of the Lamb has come, and his Bride has made herself ready; it was granted her to clothe herself with fine linen, bright and pure"— for the fine linen is the righteous deeds of the saints. And the angel said to me, "Write this: Blessed are those who are invited to the marriage supper of the Lamb."*
>
> **Revelation 19:6-9, ESV**

Our highest allegiance is to Christ. So important is this relationship in the Christian life that the New Testament refers to Him as the groom and His Church as the Bride. In the end, there will be a great union between Jesus and His people. This event will be so climatic that it is described as the marriage supper of the Lamb, and all who are invited are deeply blessed.

The benefits of marriage, like companionship and security, will be completely found in Jesus. It'll also be partially found in the people of Heaven. Heaven is a place of perfect redemption. There will be no relational strife at all. Therefore, there will be no lack of companionship or need for security.

Do people in Heaven know what's presently happening on Earth?

This is a question that has piqued curiosity and has been the subject of different media portrayals of Heaven. We have to wonder what we will be aware of on Earth. This is especially true because our hearts and minds will be so overwhelmed with the glory of God that we have to wonder if we will even care what is happening to those who remain on Earth. The Bible is pretty clear on this subject.

We have many reasons to believe that those in Heaven do know what is happening on earth. The first is that all of Heaven seems to know what is going on on Earth. God is said many times in the Psalms to be watching the actions of man. Jesus teaches that the angels rejoice when someone places their faith in Jesus. The angels are also sent to Earth to participate in spiritual warfare and to do the will of God. If every other being in Heaven is aware of the happenings on Earth, it would make sense that mankind does as well.

On top of that logical reasoning, there are passages of Scripture that point to this reality as well. This passage in Hebrews is the most convincing on the subject.

Therefore, since we are surrounded by so great a cloud of witnesses, let us also lay aside every weight, and sin which clings so closely, and let us run with endurance the race that is set before us, looking to Jesus, the founder and perfecter of our faith, who for the joy that was set before him endured the cross, despising the shame, and is seated at the right hand of the throne of God.

Hebrews 12:1-2, ESV

This passage begins a chapter often referred to as the "Hall of Faith." Person after person is mentioned in the Old and New Testaments that showed incredible faith in God. These people are the "great cloud of witnesses" that surround us as we "run the race" of the Christian life. If you can imagine a stadium filled with people with a track in the center of the arena, that is the picture the author of Hebrews is painting.

We can press on in the Christian life with endurance in our faith, knowing that our forefathers are cheering us on. We can look to their example and say with confidence that if God could use them in such a mighty way, He can use our efforts, too.

Finally, it's important to note that knowing what God is accomplishing on Earth while we're in Heaven will only serve to bring Him more glory. Think about it. We would give such honor and praise as we got to hear the heart and mind of God explain the hand of God in His orchestration of events for the day. The grace and mercy, as well as the judgment and justice that He displays throughout our lives, would bring Him more and more glory as more and more people know and understand it.

What Will We Spend Our Time Doing?

This is the ultimate question. What will we do when we get there? We've addressed this in a few different ways in this book, but let me summarize the basic teaching of Scripture here. In Heaven, we will worship, work, and wonder. We have established in one entire chapter that Heaven is a place of perfect worship.

You are the Lord, you alone. You have made heaven, the heaven of heavens, with all their host, the earth and all that is on it, the seas and all that is in them; and you preserve all of them; and the host of heaven worships you.

Nehemiah 9:6, ESV

Without any doubt, Heaven will be a place where we worship God for all of eternity. But I don't think that is all we will do. In fact, I think we have plenty of reasons to think otherwise. I think that we will all have jobs in Heaven. The first reason we ought to think that is because that was God's original, good design. When God created the Heavens and the Earth and all that is in them, he gave Adam and Eve a job to do. They were to be fruitful and multiply and have dominion over the earth.

If work is in the original design of God for mankind, why would He remove that part of our design in Heaven. After all, the New Heaven and New Earth are mirrors of the Garden of Eden anyway. We are even told in Scripture one of the jobs that we will have.

The saying is trustworthy, for: If we have died with him, we will also live with him; if we endure, we will also reign with him; if we deny him, he also will deny us; if we are faithless, he remains faithful— for he cannot deny himself.

2 Timothy 2:12-13, ESV

The promise of the Bible is that all who place their faith in Jesus will ultimately reign with Jesus. This promise of reigning takes us back to the original command of exercising dominion over the earth that was given to Adam and Eve in the Garden of Eden. What exactly we will do as a part of our reign or dominion is debatable. Perhaps the giftings that God gave us as a part of His church on Earth will be similar to our giftings in Heaven. Regardless of what it looks like, we can be assured that we will have a job that brings fulfillment and joy to our lives with Him.

We will worship, work, and wonder. Our time in glory will be like an eternal education. As has been alluded to before, now we will see in the Scripture. We will hear of and wonder at what God has done.

In the coming ages, God will show His people the immeasurable riches of His grace. He will explain to us in incredible detail all that went into the crossing of the Red Sea led by Moses. He will let us glory in how He fed 5,000 people with just a little boy's lunch. He will explain to us how he decided to create the earth with the order and design that He did. Forever and ever, we will learn of His wondrous grace.

Friend, we will worship God forever. Just for simply knowing Him in His glory, we will be drawn to worship Him with each passing moment. We will work for God forever, not in a dead-end job that brings no joy, but in a job that is tailor-made for our skill set. And we will wonder at the work of God forever. Over and over again, we will learn something new about our incredible Savior, God, and King.

ON EARTH AS IT IS IN HEAVEN

You may be tempted to be frustrated by what you don't know about Heaven. I want to encourage you to rejoice at what you don't know by looking at it in a different light. If we understood all that Heaven was and all that we would do there, it would be a pretty small place.

It has taken humanity thousands of years to scratch the surface of the Earth. We have learned of the vast amounts of animals and insects. We have explored countless mountains and dived into the deepest parts of the oceans. Even still, we have yet to learn a fraction of what this Earth holds. If this is true of our temporary home, imagine how much more it is true of our Heavenly home. Do not be disappointed in what we don't know yet. Let that wonder fuel your desire to see it for yourself.

Embrace the unique things you can learn and discover here on Earth. Don't let your curiosity die. There is so much to do and see. But let that curiosity be because of a deeper one. Let it be there because you're anticipating a more wonderful place to discover. The beauties of Earth and its mysteries will be nothing in comparison to the perfect, eternal home for all who believe in Jesus.

CONCLUSION

What a glorious future we have in store. Just the thought of it can make your desire to be with Christ well up to the point where you're shouting with Paul, " For to me to live is Christ, and to die is gain. If I am to live in the flesh, that means fruitful labor for me. Yet which I shall choose, I cannot tell. I am hard-pressed between the two. My desire is to depart and be with Christ, for that is far better" (Philippians 1:21-23). So what do we do until that glorious day when we are called home through death, or Jesus returns?

In Mark Chapter 4, Jesus lays out for us what we are to do for the sake of the kingdom until it is on earth as it is in Heaven. Let's take a look.

Again he began to teach beside the sea. And a very large crowd gathered about him, so that he got into a boat and sat in it on the sea, and the whole crowd was beside the sea on the land. And he was teaching them many things in parables, and in his teaching he said to them: "Listen! Behold, a sower went out to sow. And as he sowed, some seed fell along the path, and the birds came and devoured it. Another seed fell on rocky ground, where it did not have much soil, and immediately it sprang up, since it had no depth of soil. And when the sun rose, it was scorched, and since it had no root, it withered away. Other seed fell among thorns, and the thorns grew up and choked it, and it yielded no grain. And other

Advertisements are everywhere. In fact, on your way to work today, you heard one on your radio. You passed a billboard or a sign. You saw something on Facebook. But what makes you actually go try a new store or a new restaurant? A good picture of a hamburger might get you to McDonald's, but if someone comes up to you and tells you how good it is, you'll remember that.

In our text this morning, there are no signs, radios, or Facebook ads necessary for Jesus' ministry to continue to expand. Word of mouth has taken over, and people are flocking to him. The point Jesus makes about the kingdom of God is this: We should spread the word to grow the kingdom.

Mark's Gospel account is known for its fast-paced, action-packed narra-tive. In the first three chapters, you'll read about five miracles in detail, and countless others have been referenced. But in this passage at hand, we come to one of only two extended recordings of Jesus' teaching.

We have Chapter 4, containing various parables. And we have chapter 13 considering the end-times. Since these sections of extended teaching are sparse, we should perk up our ears to hear what is being taught. These sections must be foundational to understanding who Jesus is.

We all know someone who is soft-spoken, but when they speak, they have something of immense value to share. This is that moment for us in Mark. So, let's dig in and decipher this all-important parable for ourselves.

This scene should be all too familiar to us at this point: Jesus teaching by the sea of Galilee. Standing in a boat between two hills, there is a natural amphitheater where He is teaching the crowd that has gathered once again. Notice the first word, "Hearken." This is the first time He called for the attention of the people in this way. It's more forceful than, "Listen up!" It carries the weight of Scriptures like Deuteronomy 6:4: "Hear, O Israel: the Lord our God is one Lord."

With a prophetic voice, He commands the attention of His followers to share the parable of the sower. Immediately when we read a parable, we will be tempted to start determining for ourselves what each thing represents. Early in my preaching days, I got called out for this. In preparing a lesson on Jesus' teachings on building a house on the rock or on the sand, I was talking with my dad about my thoughts. He lovingly and gently rebuked my interpretation. Instead of looking to the Word for interpretation, I looked to my own thoughts and cleverness.

Graciously, Jesus has given us the interpretation of this passage. We don't have to guess what the seed is or what the soil is. The Seed is the Word (Mark 4:14). What word? Is this a reference to the Word of God as a whole? Or is there something specific in mind? Let's look at Mark as a whole to find our answer.

Jesus came in preaching the gospel of the kingdom of God (Mark 1:14). He preached "the word" (Mark 2:2), pointing to Him as the Son of Man, the King of the kingdom of God. Even in the former chapter, we can read about Him defending a united kingdom (Mark 3:24). While there is the application for us to sow the Word of God as a whole, in the parable, Jesus is pinpointing the idea of the gospel of the kingdom of God.

In essence, we're getting an origin story. How will the kingdom of God begin to grow? How will Jesus usher in the kingdom of God? By sowing the word. It will happen by preaching the same Gospel message that Jesus has been preaching from the beginning. While there are four types of soil, there is only one type of seed. Only one message He will bring.

Friend, this is what I hope will be true in your life. Whoever shares with you from the Word of God, I pray that only one type of seed will go out. The seed of self-help will not grow in the kingdom of God. The seed of salvation that is in limbo based on how good you were that day will not grow in the kingdom. The seed of naming it and claiming it will not grow the kingdom. Only the seed of the gospel of the kingdom of God will do the work.

It is the gospel that is "the power of God for salvation to everyone who believes." (Romans 1:16). The gospel is the message we have received, in which we now stand, and by which we are being saved (1 Corinthians 15:1-2). The gospel is our very strength (Romans 16:25). The kingdom of God will be grown by the gospel. Let's take a look now at those who will hear the gospel.

THE SOIL

And he said to them, "Do you not understand this parable? How then will you understand all the parables? The sower sows the word. And these are the ones along the path, where the word is sown: when they hear, Satan immediately comes and takes away the word that is sown in them. And these are the ones sown on rocky ground: the ones who, when they hear the word, immediately receive it with joy. And they have no root in themselves, but endure for a while; then, when tribulation or persecution arises on account of the word, immediately they fall away. And others are the ones sown among thorns. They are those who hear the word, but the cares of the world and the deceitfulness of riches and the desires for other things enter in and choke the word, and it proves unfruitful. But those that were sown on the good soil are

Before we get into the soil, let's notice the process of sowing. If you're
agriculturally minded, you may be thinking to yourself that this guy
has no idea how to sow the seed! Look at him! He's tossing it all over
the place. He's done nothing to prepare the soil! Shouldn't it hill till the
land? Shouldn't he dig out the rocks and pull the weeds? This form of
sowing seed is how they did it back then. They would toss the seed on
the ground and manually push each seed into the ground with a stick.

Don't get the wrong image in your mind of a sower who is lazy or in-
competent. In fact, we ought to be deeply encouraged by this sower.
Regardless of the state of the soil, the seed went out. Friends, we don't
get to pick and choose who is worthy of hearing the Gospel message.
We don't get to decide based on how someone looks whether or not
they will be receptive. Go out to the yard beside the church and take a
long, hard look. Can you tell me where the rocks are just by looking at
the surface? Neither can we tell who has a tender heart ready to receive
the Gospel.

I think we can use this as an excuse for not sharing the Gospel. We think
to ourselves, "They wouldn't accept it anyway. What's the point?" The
point is that the gospel is the power of God to save all men. Brother or
sister, don't be a stingy sower. Liberally, share the Gospel with every
chance you get.

Let's see how the soils are described by Jesus. The first is on the wayside, like a well-walked trail through the woods. The ground would be
so hard that the seed would stand no chance of being pushed through.
In this case, the heart is so hard that it won't even grasp the Word. Satan
swoops in like a bird to steal it away.

The next is the stony soil. The soil is so filled with rocks that the roots have nowhere to grow and grain strength. This is a picture of the heart that hears the word and has a "temporary faith." They show initial signs of saving faith but fall away when life gets hard.

Next is the thorny soil. Soil is so crowded with other growth that there isn't room for the new growth to thrive. It gets choked out. This is a picture of the heart who hears the word, but the cares of the world speak louder in their ears, and they fall away. Perhaps the Prodigal Son (Luke 15:11-32) before his return home is a good picture of this person.

Finally, there is the Good Soil. The soil was so good that the harvest was nearly miraculous. The farmer on this day was hoping for an average harvest of 10 fold, but this type of seed in the good soil was good for at least 30 fold and up to 100 fold.

Why is Jesus giving us this parable? Does He want us to be soil inspectors? Looking into people's lives before we share the word? Is He giving us a spiritual growth test? Calling us to remove rocks and thorns from our souls? While there is some merit to applying this passage in this way, the bigger point Jesus is making here is this: His kingdom is going to begin this way. A lot of sown seed. Only a few plots of good soil. And those with receptive hearts are going to expand in a miraculous way.

You see, Jesus has already been sowing seed on all kinds of soil. You have the wayside of the scribes who were so hardened that they would rather believe Jesus' power to be from Satan than from God. You have the stony soil of the crowds who were eager to hear His word, but they will not endure the hardships of following Him. You have the thorny soil of people like the rich young ruler who was obedient to the law but unwilling to give up his riches to follow Jesus. Finally, you have the good soil, which was the hundreds (and at points thousands) of people following Him. We know of 11 that followed Him to the end.

And from those few came the church as we know it today. With untold numbers, that good soil produced an incredible harvest! Isn't this wonderful, Church? That Jesus would give us not only the parable but the explanation as well? We can understand all that He has to say because we have both pieces of the puzzle. But that wasn't the case for the crowds. Not everyone at this time was clued in.

THE SECRET

And when he was alone, those around him with the twelve asked him about the parables. And he said to them, "To you has been given the secret of the kingdom of God, but for those outside everything is in parables, so that "'they may indeed see but not perceive, and may indeed hear but not understand, lest they should turn and be forgiven.'"

Mark 4:10-13, ESV

At first glance, it seems as if Jesus doesn't want the crowds to turn and be forgiven! Has He condemned them already? Will He leave them out of His offer of salvation? Surely not! Jesus' own words in John 3:16 say otherwise. "For God so loved the world that whosoever will believe will not perish but have eternal life."

Jesus here is cultivating good soil. He knows that, ultimately, the disciples will see and perceive. They will hear and understand. They will turn and be forgiven, while the crowds will not. He pulls the 12 men to the side and says, "You've been brought into the inside. I'm going to share with you the secret." Although they were given special insight into what Jesus meant, they didn't fully understand. Mark 6:52 describes their reaction to Jesus walking on water as hard-hearted. Mark 8:18 describes their reaction to a bread shortage as "having eyes and they do not see." Even after 3 years of intimate ministry with Jesus, Judas Iscariot would betray Him.

It's not until the cross of Christ that the message and ministry of Christ can be fully understood. Have you noticed all of the times when Jesus tells the people not to spread the word about His miracles? He said this to the demons in Mark 1:34. Not long after this, He said it to the leper in Mark 1:44. And again He said it to the demons in Mark 3:12.

Why? We're given insight in John 6:15. After feeding the 5,000, Jesus "[perceived] that they were about to come and take him by force to make him king, Jesus withdrew again to the mountain by himself." Jesus' plan from before the foundation of the world was to go to the cross. This is the very reason He came, to give His life as a ransom for many. So, this "secret of the Kingdom" had to stay that way until the right time.

Maybe you're reading this, and you're worried. Is there any hope for my son? My neighbor? My spouse? Because they sound a lot like the way side, the stony soil, or the thorny soil. Soil can't change itself, so is there any hope? Friend, read this closely. Our God is a gardener.

He can plow the hardest earth, remove the largest of stones, and pluck every painful thorn from our souls. You see, His Son, Jesus, was raised up from this hard earth bearing a crown of thorns only to be killed and placed behind a stone. None of those things held Him back then, and they won't hold Him back now. Keep sowing that seed! And see the kingdom of God grow on earth as it is in Heaven. Until we die or Jesus returns, we are to grow the kingdom by spreading the seed of God's Word. Not only this, but we are to be living in light of the kingdom coming.

What are you excited about? What are you anticipating? Maybe you're anticipating the simple things in life. Settling into the couch and turning on a Seinfeld rerun? Maybe another playoff win for your favorite sports team. Maybe the Easter season or Sunrise Service on Easter morning. Maybe a vacation is coming up, or a grandbaby is on the way.

My son has joined Scouts, and we're getting excited about the Pinewood Derby. But if all we did was get excited about it, we'd never win the race. Our excitement is naturally going to lead us to sand, paint, watch YouTube videos, and prepare his car. In the rest of Mark 4, Jesus' message is very clear. The kingdom is coming. And our excitement about it ought to push us to action. We must do kingdom work until the kingdom comes.

In the first part of Mark 4, Jesus summarized His ministry for us. He's like a sower, sowing seed liberally. The seed of the word will fall on all types of soil. Only the good soil, plowed by the hand of God, will respond in faith. The kingdom of God is going to be made up of people like this.

Let's pause for a moment and see the end goal of this all. What does the Bible teach about the final kingdom of God? A quick walkthrough of Revelation shows us some incredible things. Rev. 11:15 says that the kingdom of the world has become the kingdom of our Lord and of his Christ, and he shall reign forever and ever. Whatever kingdom this world has to offer will not stand up to the power of our Lord.

One day, Jesus will fully establish His kingdom here. Revelation 14:3 calls it a place filled with endless worship. Revelation 19:11-13 gives us a picture of our warrior King. Revelation 21:1-5 shows us a recreated kingdom that serves to take us back to the garden of Eden.

Church, this kingdom of God is at hand! And even here now! Reigning in the hearts of every believer is our King, Jesus. And so we live in this in-between moment. Many theologians will call this an already-but-not-yet truth of Scripture.

Jesus is King now. His kingdom has begun now. But Jesus is yet to come back as King. His Kingdom has yet to be fully realized. And so, the question we're seeking to answer in the final part of Mark 4 is, what do we do until the kingdom comes? What is the kingdom work? Lift Jesus, Rely on Jesus, and Share Jesus until the kingdom comes.

> *And he said to them, "Is a lamp brought in to be put under a basket, or under a bed, and not on a stand? For nothing is hidden except to be made manifest; nor is anything secret except to come to light. If anyone has ears to hear, let him hear." And he said to them, "Pay attention to what you hear: with the measure you use, it will be measured to you, and still more will be added to you. For to the one who has, more will be given, and from the one who has not, even what he has will be taken away."*
>
> **Mark 4:21-25, ESV**

If you were to ask the question, "What is a candle for?" today, you'd get all kinds of answers. Some people would say that it is for decoration. Others would say it is to make a room smell good. Still, others might say that it is for ambiance. Ironically, only some might just say it can be used for light.

But in biblical days, this was their purpose. You'd buy a candle, or more likely, an oil lamp, and that would be used to light your home. So, where do you put your candle if that's its purpose? Wherever its light can be seen. No one would hide the candle. No one would cover it up.

If Jesus is the candle, and the gospel of the kingdom of God is the light, then what is Jesus trying to say about the kingdom in this parable? I think it's simply this: the secret of the kingdom will be revealed to all mankind. This happened in part at the cross. Mark 15:33-39 says that Jesus cried with a loud voice and gave up the ghost. And the veil of the temple was rented in twain from the top to the bottom. And when the centurion, which stood over him, saw that he so cried out and gave up the ghost, he said, Truly this man was the Son of God.

In that moment, 1 Corinthians 2:10 happened to the centurion. The Spirit revealed to Him the truth. But this hasn't happened for all men yet. Not all know the truth. But will it happen? Philippians 2:9-11 says, "Therefore God has highly exalted him and bestowed on him the name that is above every name, so that at the name of Jesus every knee should bow, in heaven and on earth and under the earth, and every tongue confess that Jesus Christ is Lord, to the glory of God the Father."

However, this revelation will not lead to the salvation of all men. But in this moment, when the kingdom finally comes, God's people will rejoice, and the rest of the world will fall down in terror of the judgment to come. There are those who have heard and will be given more at the coming of Jesus, but to those who have heard and not received Him, that opportunity will be taken away.

Imagine for a moment that I invite you to a pickup basketball game at the park. Imagine I tell you that I'm good friends with Michael Jordan and he's gonna come. What are you going to do? Not show up because you think I'm crazy? Show up because you think I'm crazy? Or tell all your friends, because if it's true, that'll be crazy!

Friend, make no mistake. Jesus is coming! But I believe that we treat that news the same as if our friend claimed to know Michael Jordan. We brush it off. We don't take it seriously. We cover the light of Christ with all kinds of baskets and beds. Unbelief that Jesus really could come back at any moment. Our business can make us so focused on building our own little kingdom.

Friend, let's lift Jesus high until the Kingdom comes. Let it be at the top of your mind by digging into the word daily. Pause to honor King Jesus in the business of life by personal prayer or by giving up some of your rest time to grab dinner or coffee with someone. Do good works and use them as an avenue to share the gospel. In everything, lift Jesus high. Not only are we to lift Jesus, but we are also to rely on Him.

And he said, "The kingdom of God is as if a man should scatter seed on the ground. He sleeps and rises night and day, and the seed sprouts and grows; he knows not how. The earth produces by itself, first the blade, then the ear, then the full grain in the ear. But when the grain is ripe, he puts in the sickle, because the harvest has come."

Mark 4:26-29, ESV

I love this parable. It gives me so much hope and encouragement when it comes to ministry: "the seed should spring and grow up, he knoweth not how." Don't you love those moments in your life? God, I don't know how you managed to pull me through this! I don't know how I ended up here! I don't know what I was thinking about trying that! In contrast to the parable of the sower that notices the different kinds of soils, here we have a parable focused on the reliance on the sower.

Can any gardener force their plants to grow? You can provide the best soil, regular watering, and even set up a chair and cheer it on every day of its life, but who determines its growth? It's not the gardener, nor is it the seed. God must grow it! Psalm 127:1 says, "Unless the Lord builds the house, they labor in vain to build it." 1 Corinthians 3:6 says, "I have planted, Apollos watered, but God gave the increase." The kingdom of God is built through the efforts of man. It is not reliant on them. Rather, any effort made on our behalf to build the Kingdom that isn't reliant on God is wasted.

What do Jesus' reliant efforts look like? It looks like the grandparents are earnestly praying for their children's salvation even though they are far from God. It looks like the exhausted employees singing "It is well with my soul" on their way to another long day at work. It looks like the parent of a soldier starting each day by saying, "God, I trust you with their life."

It looks like giving sacrificially to meet the needs of another. It looks like making care bags or working on a home, even though you personally may not get to speak with the people you've helped. It looks like picking your child up and flying them around the room like Superman. They can hold their arms out and will themselves to fly all they want, but until you pick them up, there is no flight. Until we step into Heaven, we must lift Jesus high, rely on Him, and share His message with the world.

SHARE JESUS UNTIL THE KINGDOM COMES

And he said, "With what can we compare the kingdom of God, or what parable shall we use for it? It is like a grain of mustard seed, which, when sown on the ground, is the smallest of all the seeds on earth, yet when it is sown it grows up and becomes larger than all the garden plants and puts out large branches, so that the birds of the air can make nests in its shade." With many such parables he spoke the word to them, as they were able to hear it. He did not speak to them without a parable, but privately to his own disciples he explained everything.

Mark 4:30-34, ESV

Some critical scholars have tried to claim that the Bible is not reliable because of this parable. Jesus makes the statement that the mustard seed is "less than all the seeds of the earth." The Jewel Orchid seed is 0.05mm in length, which is 20x smaller than a mustard seed. However, Jesus isn't trying to teach a science lesson. He's trying to make a point: out of something so small will come something of incredible size.

We're talking about exponential growth beyond the millionth degree. From a ballpoint on a pen to this massive tree, so the kingdom of God will grow. And this has happened! Starting with 1 man and His 12 disciples became 72 disciples (Luke 10), which became 120 disciples (Acts 1), which became 3000 more (Acts 2), and today, there are reported to be 2.3 Billion worldwide (Pew Research). That's not counting the innumerable that have existed between Pentecost and today. And it surely hasn't considered how many there are to come!

God told Abraham in Genesis 15:5 to look up in the sky and count the stars. That's how big my kingdom will be. Friend, we cannot be satisfied, even with these incredible numbers. Although the kingdom of God is already massive, we want more. The Lord is still on a mission! Don't let those numbers fool you because the kingdom may be small where you live.

How can we reach people for the kingdom? The way we're going to reach them is by personal and corporate evangelism. Personally, each one of us must be like missionaries in our neighborhoods, workplaces, and families. Corporately, we have to share the gospel through our events at our local church. Brothers and sisters, we must share Jesus until the kingdom comes.

And I love the picture of rest that is presented here: a tree so big that it can provide rest for the birds. So the kingdom of God will be: So expansive, so all-encompassing that there will be ample rest to all who find refuge in its shade. Ezekiel 17:23-24 "On the mountain height of Israel will I plant it, that it may bear branches and produce fruit and become a noble cedar. And under it will dwell every kind of bird; in the shade of its branches, birds of every sort will nest. And all the trees of the field shall know that I am the Lord; I bring down the high tree, and make high the low tree, dry up the green tree, and make the dry tree flourish. I am the Lord; I have spoken, and I will do it."

Friend, a wonderful pastor, and theologian, once said, "It is the task of the church to make the invisible kingdom visible." Are you doing that kingdom work? Are you lifting Jesus high? Are you relying on His grace each day? Are you sharing Him with others?

Have you ever waited for a baby's arrival? It's a wonderful and scary time in your life when you learn that there is a baby on the way! After the shock and joy begin to wane, you realize all that needs to be done before the baby arrives. You have to prepare a nursery. There are mountains of clothes to buy. The house has to be baby-proofed. This list goes on and on. We build their little kingdom, but it's not complete until they arrive. Friend, we must do kingdom work until the kingdom comes.

I've been thinking about death a lot lately. Don't get too worried about me. I'm too young for a mid-life crisis (according to Google), and I don't have enough money to enjoy one (according to my bank account). But death has been on my mind in a way that it never has before.

This is partly due to what I am teaching in my church. For the past few weeks, on Wednesday nights, we've been discussing the topic of Heaven based on a few passages of Scripture. The brilliance of the throne of God in Revelation 4, the worthiness of the Lamb in Revelation 5, and all things new to come in Revelation 21 have been incredible to behold. But implicit in the entire study is the curse of death.

But even before this study with my church family, I noticed this new focus as I was watching a hospital drama with Hannah. Never before has viewing the passing of someone on television really affected me. But now, things are different. With each episode, I have been more presently reminded of the fragility of life and the loss experienced in death. Whether it's the thought of my own death or the death of someone I love, it feels like a pit in my stomach. The weight of the loss is unbearable to consider.

And that's what death is, right? A loss. It's a loss of life. It's a loss of loved ones. It's a loss of opportunity. It's a loss of hugs. It's a loss of laying in bed watching hospital dramas with the love of your life. This is why I am puzzled by how Paul describes death.

Christ will be honored in my body, whether by life or by death. For to me to live is Christ, and to die is gain. If I am to live in the flesh, that means fruitful labor for me. Yet which I shall choose

I confess to you that death does not feel like gain. When that reality enters my thoughts, I flee in fear of the loss it brings. I have wrestled with this and will continue to do so. But as I've meditated on this passage of Scripture and others, I've come to a conclusion. Death ought not to be the focus of my thoughts, but Christ. It is the honor of Christ that is seen in the life of Paul and will be gained all the more in his death. When pressed hard between life and death, Paul desires to depart (through death) in order to be with Christ. Death has no sting in the mind of Paul because of Christ (1 Corinthians 15:56-57).

Until Jesus returns and removes death altogether (Revelation 21:4), it cannot be ignored. But it must not be the end of the thoughts of the Christian. Brothers and sisters, it is right to weep over the loss of death. But never without those tears being wiped away by our Savior.

Acknowledgments

✓ ESV Bible

✓ Come Thou Fount of Every Blessing by Robert Robinson

✓ On Jordan's Stormy Banks by Samuel Stennett

✓ Gary Thomas, in Christianity Today,
   October 3, 1994, p. 26. - Hope chapter

www.ingramcontent.com/pod-product-compliance
Lightning Source LLC
LaVergne TN
LVHW011922160726
843514LV00004B/891